The Journey
to a
Little White House

Anecdotes of Lessons Learned

Lynda M. Buckman

 FriesenPress

One Printers Way
Altona, MB R0G 0B0
Canada

www.friesenpress.com

ISBN
978-1-03-918267-7 (Hardcover)
978-1-03-918266-0 (Paperback)
978-1-03-918268-4 (eBook)

1. FAMILY & RELATIONSHIPS, FRIENDSHIP

Distributed to the trade by The Ingram Book Company

To my three Children
and their Dad
– Thanks for all the great memories!

Introduction

On a warm spring day in 1967, my boyfriend and I were sitting on a small park bench talking about the future we would have together. We shared a dream about having a little white house in the country. We decided that it would be beside a stream and have a white picket fence. We would have a small dog for me and a big dog for him.

As the conversation progressed, I suggested that it was all quite fine but that we weren't even engaged yet! My boyfriend immediately stood up from the bench, got down on one knee and proposed. I said "yes", and our lives were joined forever because of our dream of a little white house.

This is our story. I wanted to write about the experiences in our life that brought us to where we are today. Most of what I learned in my early life was through the things that I did. Once I was married, I learned from the various aspects of the life we shared as we grew together. Both of us brought different experiences into each venture and eventually we began to think alike as we continued to learn.

We were both in the Royal Canadian Navy in our early adult years. We were born into vastly different environments but the Military trained us to think and act in the same way. This became the basis of our life together and created a way of maintaining a strong relationship for the rest of our lives. When asked for the reason that we have been married for 55 years, the answer has always been that we had the same Military training.

My father was a Military man and I spent the first 30 years of my life living with the Military in one way or another. My father taught me many things about life and gave great advice that I have used throughout the years. His philosophy was that you should try everything you encounter, at least once. You should never say you can't to something unless you have tried it first and that everyone can do everything, but often at different levels. Always go your own way and look out for "Number 1".

The last piece of advice he gave me, before I left home for my career in the Navy, was "Never marry a sailor!" This was the only piece of advice he gave me that I intentionally ignored.

I eventually left the Military to marry my husband, a Navy sailor. We shared many good times as a couple, had lots of adventures and when our first son arrived we were ready for family life and our dream of a little white house slipped away into the many stories of our past.

Our journey unintentionally changed many times. As we moved from one place to the next, our life and our focus was altered. Each of the Parts in this story tells of a change in our life and each house we lived in became a milestone that carried us forward on a new path. The anecdotes are about the lessons we learned along the way.

This story began when we were posted to a Military Base in the lower mainland of British Columbia, a couple of years before our first son was born. We were posted many times over the years until finally my husband was released from the Navy. Once out of the Navy, we entered the world of civilian life which my husband had long since left behind and I had never known. As we embarked on a life of independence and business, we were free to make our own choices about where and how we lived. Life wasn't always easy but we always made our choices together and worked hard at whatever we chose. Sometimes we had to learn the hard way but we still learned from everything we did.

This book is about what we learned together and about all the different things we tried. We never looked back or wished things were different. We faced every challenge that came our way. Three things that remained consistent in these times were our children, our pets, and livestock and this story is what these anecdotes are mostly about. They were interesting and fun times with a few surprises thrown in.

Today, we are retired, with no kids, no pets, and no livestock. Our three children are all grown and married with children and pets of their own and we are now the proud grandparents of ten grandchildren: five boys and five girls. Our oldest son works on a farm and is the only one who has adventures with livestock these days.

Contents

PART 1
A TALE OF THREE HOUSES
The Military Base (House #1)

This was the first time we had been "posted" as a married couple. So, we were moving to a Military Base in a new town on the mainland. We packed up our belongings and two dogs and boarded a ferry to the mainland. Our furniture would arrive shortly after us.

We had been assigned a rental house in the "Permanent Married Quarters" near the Military Base outside of town. We had no idea what to expect. We had never lived in "Permanent Married Quarters" before. We had friends living in "PMQs" but we had always rented our own accommodations. Actually, it never crossed our minds to try to obtain PMQ accommodation. Now that was where we were going to live.

Permanent Married Quarters (PMQs)

There were about fifty PMQ houses on the Base. They were smaller than we imagined since the PMQs our friends had lived in on the island were much larger. Our house was a one storey, one bedroom, no basement house on the corner of the street. The small street was horseshoe shaped and lined with houses on both sides. Most of the families were about our age, some with children and their husbands would be working on the Base with my husband.

Life in the PMQs took a little getting used to. There were people and kids around all the time and everyone was on a schedule according to the shifts of the husbands. We were land based now so there were no cruises on Destroyers which meant that we had a lot of time to ourselves for a change. We did more visiting with relatives who lived on the mainland, we had new friends and a lot more shopping in the new stores we had never been in.

My days were my own when my husband was on the day or afternoon shifts because I didn't have a job for the first time since we were married. I made a lot of friends on the Base. I was able to have coffee during the day with the other wives and we partied with other families on the weekends. It all seems so nice, ideal for a while.

However, I had some problems with the other women on the Base. They had groups and were very cliquey. All I had to do was say the wrong thing at the wrong time and trouble ensued. All of a sudden, I would be uninvited to afternoon coffee or a "Tupperware" party and I didn't even know what I had done. They would never even tell you what was wrong, you just weren't part of the group anymore. I soon realized that this was the normal life in PMQs. My husband found the same problem at work. If I was 'out' so was he, and if he was 'out' so was I. When he got a promotion and the other guy didn't, you were ignored by that group. This was not the way we wanted to live, but right then we had no other choice, so we learned to make the best of it. **Lesson Learned!**

The Arrival Of The Piano

When I was a child, my parents decided to buy a piano. There were four girls in the family and they decided that who ever showed an interest would be given piano lessons. The piano was a Gerard Heinzman, upright grand with a full steel harp. It was beautiful and I loved to play on it. I had no musical talent but it didn't matter. I was the only one who showed any interest so I received eight years of piano lessons. I learned to read music and how to play but was never going to be a pianist. Eventually, I was good enough to entertain relatives at Christmas and to play most of the family favorites.

When I left home, my life moving around in the Navy did not make the piano an asset so it stayed with my parents. I never thought of it as mine anyway, it belonged to my parents. When we moved to the mainland, near to where my parents lived, my mother asked me if I would like to have the piano. I was thrilled.

My parents arranged to have the piano shipped to us on the Base. Our house was small but we didn't have a lot of furniture so we had enough room for it. The piano arrived in a few days, while my husband was at work, with two men to unload it. However, there was a problem!

The entrance through the front door was easy enough, but once through the door, the men had to turn the piano ninety degrees and that was impossible because of its length. After some discussion, they decided to put it on its end and slide it in and then turn it. Once through the door, they turned the piano partly, but now it still wouldn't go through the second doorway because the legs on it stuck out too far. They checked the back door of the house and decided it was just as bad. Tried as they might, it appeared that there was no way it would go through the front or back door. I suggested they take it back to my parents. They said, "No!", and then they left the piano on its end, in the front doorway, got into their truck and departed without even saying "Goodbye". I was left standing in the doorway with the piano upended and unable to close the front door.

When my husband came home, he was flabbergasted that any delivery company would do that. After some unreasonable options were discussed, we settled on cutting the legs off so that it could be turned and slid into the living room. We could reattach the legs, but the piano would never be the same. Once the legs were off, the piano slid easily into the living room and we reattached the legs. My husband enlisted a couple of friends to help turn the piano back onto its newly attached legs and all was well. It would have to be checked over and tuned but it looked good in our living room. We had learned that whenever we moved in the future, we should be careful to assess the doorways before the piano was moved. **Lesson Learned!**

The Laundry Stoop

With the piano repaired and in place, we settled into a somewhat normal routine. My husband's schedule pretty much dictated my schedule. It was quite satisfying having regular hours every day. It made planning a lot easier.

My schedule now included hanging laundry on the clothesline every few days. I had never had a clothesline before and I loved the fresh smell of laundry dried in the open air. Every Base house had a clothesline in the backyard.

We really didn't have a 'backyard' though. The back of our house faced a large rectangle of open field that was the backyard to all the houses facing inward on the horseshoe shaped street. The field was well worn and quite scruffy. There was only a little grass left and it would get quite muddy when it rained. Most of the children played in the field on the weekends and especially during their summer holidays. In any case, it was open for everyone and a lot of us used our clotheslines which extended about ten feet into the field.

Outside our back door, was a square cement slab that served as a small porch, and two steps to walk down to the yard. The porch was too small to stand on for hanging clothes and the clothesline was too high off the ground to reach to hang clothes while standing on the ground. Just inside the back door of the house was a small, rectangular stool that we imagined was meant to be used to stand on to hang clothes. The stool had to be moved outside each time and brought in when the laundry was done, but it worked well enough.

Doing laundry and putting it on the line had its hazards when it had rained all night. Dropping pins or laundry on the ground was exasperating, but it happened on occasion and usually only when the ground was muddy. Why do things like that never happen when the ground is dry?

"However," became a word that I could not ignore in my life. So...

However, one such day a new hazard struck. While pinning clothes to the line, I glanced to my side and noticed a young boy playing a short distance away. I wasn't surprised, but he was pretty much covered in mud from playing in the field. I wondered if his mother knew what a mess he was. Before I realized what was happening, he ran up to me and pulled my stoop out from under my feet. My half-full basket of laundry and I went flying into the mud on the ground. I let out a holler as I fell and the young boy turned and ran. Good thing for him that he did! By the time I gathered my wits about me, I had just enough time to see him enter one of the houses nearby. I would be giving his mother a visit and soon!

My laundry and my pins were all over the muddy ground and so was I. I wasn't hurt luckily, but I was a mess. I gathered everything up and returned to the safety of the house. What was left of the laundry had to be washed again, as well as the clothes I was wearing. My hair was caked with mud so what I really needed was a shower. Unfortunately, we didn't have a shower, so I had a long bath and then washed my hair several times in the kitchen sink.

By the time I was all cleaned up and the laundry was done, the sun was shining outside and the field was starting to dry out. I went back outside, put my stoop back in its place and finished hanging my freshly washed laundry. I kept a sharp eye out for the little rascal that upended me and anyone else in the field with 'ill-intent'.

I had a cup of coffee and settled down, then walked across the street to talk to the little boy's mother. At first she said that he hadn't been out all day, but when I told her I knew who he was, she just shrugged and said that it was an innocent prank. As I walked home, I was furious that his mother could have cared so little about what might have happened as a result of my fall. I soon realized that she just didn't care and I was wasting my time being upset and decided to just 'get over it', but I never really did.

My husband and I talked it over and we decided to build a permanent stoop and even add a clothespin holder to the side of the house. I didn't hang laundry again until it was built. Problem solved. **Lesson Learned!**

A Samoyed Husky &
A Vacuum Cleaner

While in our previous residence, our neighbour had approached us for a favor. They were moving to the mainland and had rented a temporary house but the landlord did not allow pets. They hoped to find better accommodations in the following month. They wanted us to take care of their dog for a while until they could move somewhere else.

Being good friends, we knew the dog well. It was a two-year-old spayed, female Samoyed Husky, named Tasha. She was a beautiful large white ball of fluff. When she was bathed and blow-dried she would fill the back seat of any car – especially ours! We were very fond of her, so being young and foolish, we said yes, of course. Having a dog was nothing new, we already had one and they played well together. By the time we were ready to move, they still had not found a new place to rent with a dog.

Here we were in the small Base house with two big dogs. Our dog, Kelly, was a shepherd cross and the two of them were about the same size – BIG! They were good dogs so the size of them had never been a problem. Kelly preferred being outside while Tasha seemed to prefer being inside where she could be near me.

After moving to the Base, she became even more attached to me. She followed me all over the house all day long. At first, I was flattered that she wanted my attention all the time, but eventually it became a problem. If I was making the bed, she would sit on it and stop me and I would have to give up and do something else until my husband came home to take her for a walk.

One morning while I was in the kitchen doing dishes, she continually pushed against me until she finally got between me and the sink. She was a really big dog, and it was hard to reach over top of her to get to the dishes. This novel approach she had became a game to her and doing dishes became a challenge because she would push against me until I was too far from the sink and had to stop to play with her. She usually won this game and the dishes would have to sit until later.

Then came the vacuum cleaning. We owned an Electrolux vacuum cleaner for many years. I usually vacuumed once or twice a week. In the beginning, there were no problems with this chore in my schedule, but Tasha had another game to play to get my attention. The smaller areas of the house were easy to do because she was so big that there wasn't room for both of us around the furniture, however, the hallway and the living room were a different story.

Tasha found out that the hose on the vacuum cleaner was long enough that she could sit on it when it was close to the floor and then I couldn't move the vacuum. I tried to work around this by keeping the hose off the floor as much as possible but it was not easy because the working end of the vacuum was a stiff metal 3-foot-long wand and very awkward to hold up high enough to keep the hose off the floor and away from Tasha. I actually had to take the wand off and work with just the shorter braided hose end nearest the base. I managed to get the vacuuming done most days working one way then the other and some days I just gave up altogether.

Tasha was a friendly pet to have, but she needed training that we were not interested in giving her because she was not our dog. Eventually the call came from her owners and she was returned to them, regretfully. She had become a part of our family for almost a year. When we returned her to her owners, they were extremely excited to see her when we arrived. She bounded through their front door, went right past them and straight out their open back door. We visited for a while, waiting for Tasha to be rounded up so we could say goodbye, but they couldn't find her. We finally left for home. We called a week later and were told that Tasha was never seen again. We missed her but had learned to never dog sit again. **Lesson Learned!**

The Aquarium

After Tasha was gone everything settled down again. I decided to get into selling Avon Products, increasingly popular at this time. I did quite well with regular customers all over the Base. I managed to make enough money to buy and stock a 20-gallon aquarium for our living room. We put it up against the wall under our gun rack which displayed our four rifles. We enjoyed the aquarium and had some adventures trying to keep it stocked while learning about temperatures and varied species of fish. We learned a lot about tropical fish. We had a variety of common aquarium fish from the pet store. Mollies, tetras, zebras, and angel fish were our favorites. We learned early on that some species did well and some just died in a few days. We were particularly fond of the neon tetras. They were exactly what they sound like. Flashy, bright coloured little fish that swam about the tank, darting here and there. They never really slowed down and were a lot of fun to watch.

After a few months most of our fish died off. We kept replacing them, trying to get the right combination. We finally decided to just buy a bunch of neon tetras since we liked them so much. We brought home ten for the tank since they seemed to survive the best of all our choices. They did very well at first, but we soon changed our minds about them. Within a few days, there were a couple missing, they just disappeared. A few days later and a couple more disappeared. After a chat with the pet shop, it turned out that we may have made a mistake. Apparently, lacking other species in the tank, the neon tetras were eating each other. Sure, enough in a few days there were only two left. Time to change our strategy.

We returned to the pet shop to restock the aquarium. With some advice from the owner, we came home with a couple of varieties which included some "hatchet" fish. These little fish were shaped like the head of a hatchet, hence their name. They were fun to watch as well. They would swim along the top of the surface of the water quickly and darted all over the tank. The aquarium seemed to thrive with our new choices.

However, as always, there was an unforeseen problem. The top of the aquarium was covered in two pieces. One piece was for the light and the second was a cover for the rest of the top. There was a small gap about a quarter of an inch between the two pieces. Now, we had no idea that this would cause a problem. As it happens, the hatchet fish skim along the top of the water in the aquarium, just a hair under the surface. Apparently, if they break the surface tension of the water at that speed they are tossed out of the water. Anywhere else in the tank, they would immediately fall back in the water. What are the odds that they would break the surface along this tiny little gap between the covers? Surprisingly good as it turns out. We eventually lost all five of our hatchet fish this way. Over a period of three months, we found each one of them dead on the floor in front of the aquarium. In later years we found an aquarium cover that was one piece and were able to have hatchet fish again. At this time in our life, we gave up on both neon tetras and hatchet fish and finally settled for guppies and goldfish. **Lesson Learned!**

The Aquarium & The Gun Rack

As a young couple we enjoyed partying with our friends on occasion. We weren't great party people but now and then it was fun. My husband often had occasion to party with his friends on the Base. Especially notable were celebrations for birthdays and sports events. I would get a call in the afternoon that there was going to be a 'bash' after work and not to wait up for him. Usually, he would be back about midnight when the party broke up. He seldom got really drunk, but most of the time he was a little 'tipsy'.

On one of these celebration occasions, they got into a discussion about hunting and they apparently wanted to see our rifle collection, and our piano. I have no idea how these two ideas had anything to do with each other, but that's what I was told later.

I had gone to bed at my usual time and was sound asleep. My husband woke me up at 2 am to tell me that the 'boys' wanted me to play the piano. I thought he was kidding, but he insisted. I put on my housecoat, ran a brush through my hair and walked into the living room. There was a party going on! Three or four of the guys were laughing heartily and they all greeted me in an unusually friendly manner as you can imagine considering that they had been drinking for hours.

They encouraged me to play some of their favorite tunes and in spite of their condition, they managed to sing along. After a couple of tunes, I put the cover down on the keys and accepted a round of applause. I was offered a drink but had a cola instead.

The conversation turned to the rifles on the rack above the aquarium. They spent a few minutes discussing the rifles and what they were. On the rack were a 410 shotgun, a .22 rifle, a 303 Leigh-Enfield and a 30-30 Winchester. There was continued discussion about the virtues of each model which only lasted a few minutes before one of the guys reached up and grabbed for the 30-30 Winchester. He picked it up and promptly dropped it, accidently, into the aquarium. An awful lot of excitement and confusion followed. The aquarium glass was not broken, thankfully, but the two covers on the top and the light were shattered, and a lot of water splashed all over the floor. The rifle survived as well.

The party ended abruptly. All of them turned to me, expecting an unpleasant response but I held in my frustration. They all had had too much to drink and a temper was not going to make it any better. I did suggest firmly to my husband that the party was over and maybe they should all go home. Apologies were profuse as they said good night and slinked out the door. The next day our first order of business, after assessing the damaged and cleaning up the mess, was to move the gun rack to the other wall in the living room. We should never have installed the aquarium under the gun rack in the first place. **Lesson Learned!**

Dinner With Unexpected Entertainment

After four years of marriage, we realized that we had never had my parents over for dinner. We had spent many weekends visiting them on the mainland but they had never come to the island at a time when my husband was not at sea. Now we lived only an hour away, so we decided that it was time to invite them to dinner.

My husband and I decided on a Saturday evening and planned the time and the menu. We called my parents and asked them if they would like to join us for dinner that night. They were thrilled, so we told them that dinner reservations were for 7 pm. They said that they would be delighted. We neglected to tell them that dinner was at our house. We wanted to surprise them so we let them think that we all would be going to a restaurant.

However, we did not have a dining room or even a dining area or table. Our kitchen table was barely big enough for two people and certainly not enough room in the whole kitchen to have four people and dinner. We did have a folding card table and four chairs we could use. With our small living room, it would take some careful maneuvering to set everything up comfortably but we managed to pull it off. We put up the card table and the two kitchen chairs for my parents and two folding chairs for ourselves. We did have a nice new linen tablecloth and napkins that were given to us as a wedding present which we used that evening for the first time. We also had a very appropriately small flower vase in which we put flowers for a table centre. We did not have any "fine China", so regular dishes would have to do.

We had planned ahead far enough that I had drawn up a cute sign for the front door that read "Welcome to Buck's Inn" (my husband's nickname in the Navy was "Buck"). We also planned the menu well ahead of time, so I had printed up a "Buck's Inn" menu for each of my parents. The menu included appetizers, a full course meal, beverages, and dessert. It almost looked like a real restaurant menu and we knew that they would appreciate the effort.

On Saturday night as 7 o'clock hour approached we were both nervous and excited. My parents didn't arrive early but were there shortly after 7 pm. My Dad, at first was very apologetic for being late because he thought we had dinner reservations at a restaurant for 7 pm and therefore we would obviously be late. Then he noticed the 'restaurant' sign on the door and we all had a good laugh. He was very relieved, he was never the kind of person to be late for anything, especially dinner with his daughter and her husband.

Dinner went well and without a hitch. No over-cooked or under-cooked food, everything was perfect. We enjoyed dessert and coffee. Mom and Dad were very complimentary and we were quite pleased with ourselves that everything had gone so well.

Mom and Dad moved to the chesterfield, while my husband and I cleared the table and put it away. Mom and I did the dishes while the men chatted. Then Mom and I returned to the living room for after dinner drinks. The atmosphere was very pleasant and I was glowing inside that all had gone so well. We visited with Mom and Dad for over an hour before they decided it was time to go. They thanked us for a lovely evening and were glad that we had invited them. They told us that they were particularly impressed with the effort we had gone to making the sign and the menus and asked if they could take them home. Of course, we said they could.

Just before they went out the door, my Dad thanked us for the aquarium. He said it was the most peaceful and pleasant, after dinner entertainment, he had ever had; the highlight of his evening and he would never forget it.

We learned that after all the trouble we had setting up the aquarium, the rifle incident, and the lessons on tropical fish it seemed like it had really been worth the effort. We never expected it to be the highlight of Dad's evening. **Lesson Learned!**

The Dune Buggy

It seemed to me that most boys grow up to be obsessed with cars, trucks, tractors, and anything else with wheels. My husband definitely had that trait. He was always looking for vehicular sports of one kind or another. There was a 1948 Willy's Jeep in our past that didn't quite pan out and cost me my pre-marital savings. Now with lots of spare time at home, he was looking for a new hobby. He decided that he wanted a dune buggy for some off-road adventures. Please note that "off-roading" was not a popular sport at that time and vehicles that would do that were rare. Not only did he want a dune buggy, but he wanted to build his own out of a Volkswagen. He was good enough with mechanical stuff but had never tackled anything like this and I was just young and adventurous enough to go along with the idea.

First, we needed an older, cheap Volkswagen. With a little Volkswagen research, he decided that the best Volkswagen for this purpose was a 1968 "Bug". We called every used car dealer we could find but were unsuccessful and getting disappointed. My husband was determined that it had to be a 1968 for the running gear.

During our continued search we happened to be visiting my parents. In conversation with my father, who thought we were crazy, he told us about one of the car sales outfits in town that might have a couple of Volkswagens. Anything was worth a try, so off we went. They actually had a couple of older 'Bugs' and one of them was a 1968. It wasn't all that old but it was pretty beat-up. The salesman warned us that it was not in particularly good condition. Nevertheless, my husband wanted that Bug so bad that I am certain he would have willingly pushed it the forty miles to home if he had to. We bought that junky old blue Bug for $25 and thought we got a great deal. The salesman warned us, as he gave my husband the keys, that the Bug had a 30 second, 30-foot warranty and no guarantee that the radio even worked. The warranty would last only long enough to get it off the sales lot and onto the road!

We made it off the lot and the radio worked. Great deal! We drove back to my parents house to show off our new dune-buggy in the making. Dad showed restrained enthusiasm as my husband explained what he had planned. Now he knew we were crazy, but supportive. I am certain that the 'little boy' in him wished us well and was a bit excited at the prospect of our initiative. The Bug ran quite well and we had no trouble on the way home.

Now came the demanding work. We had to install a 'stump-puller' rear end which came from a VW Van. We had no garage or other acceptable place to work on it so we set up a small workspace in the laundry room, just inside the back door. When it was installed it would provide extra power to the rear end which would be an asset while driving in the types of muddy trails we planned to explore. The installation was tricky and time consuming not to mention very messy, but it was successful.

One of our neighbours decided he wanted a dune buggy too, but he had a lot less knowledge and relied on my husband's advice on many occasions. Unfortunately, he sometimes didn't listen. He bought the wrong year for his dune buggy and when it came to installing the rear end, he put the rear end in backwards despite several warnings from my husband. The dune buggy still ran but in the process he had lowered that back end and totally defeated the purpose of the installation. He adamantly refused to discuss fixing the problem and the subject was closed but there was some satisfaction for my husband in just watching him try to back it out of his own driveway without scraping the pavement.

As the project continued, we had a problem too. The next step in our process was to cut the roof off the dune buggy. Dune buggies, I was informed, don't have roofs! OK, so cut off the roof, I told my husband. To do so, we started by taking out the back window. Since we weren't going to have a roof we also didn't need the other windows, except the windshield, so they were removed as well. The only job left was to cut all the posts between the windows and lift off the roof, which we did. Then came the most frustrating word in our vocabulary. "However," once the roof was off we realized that all the wiring that runs any Volkswagen, runs through the front drivers' window post, along the roof to the back window's post and into the trunk of the vehicle where the famous Volkswagen motor was located. We had successfully killed a Volkswagen's wiring system.

A multitude of wires now stuck up through the metal, going no where and the roof remained fully wired which was also going nowhere. It took many hours of frustration to identify and splice together all of the wires in order to run them along the floor to the back to reconnect them to the motor. There were many mistakes and frustrations but eventually the motor turned over and our dune buggy was running again. We never did get the clutch to work properly, but my husband made it work by attaching a rope to the pedal and pulling on it when he needed to change gears. To him it was a small inconvenience considering the challenge we had to get the wiring redone. We figured that maybe it would have been a clever idea to look at the wiring diagram, which we actually had, <u>before</u> we took the roof off. **Lesson Learned!**

The Mink Farm & Temptation

My Aunt and Uncle owned a mink farm only a few miles away. My husband had never been there and had only met them at our wedding. It was time for a visit. I tried to explain about how the farm worked but seeing it would be better. My Aunt and Uncle had moved from Northern Alberta several years ago and purchased many acres of farmland here. They brought their mink farm with them. We phoned ahead to set up a visit and my Aunt was excited for us to come.

My Uncle had spared no expense to build a nice house for his family which included my two male cousins, the younger was only three years older than we were and the older cousin was six years older than us. The older cousin visited frequently but remained living in Alberta. The house was built close to the road and was huge in comparison to what we were used to.

After we arrived and visited for awhile, it was time for a tour. They even had a full-sized swimming pool in the backyard that looked very inviting but would have to wait for another day as we did not have swimsuits with us. A few yards from the house was a large shed which was actually totally refrigerated and also held a feed-grinder. The mink were fed a mixture of grains and fish which arrived in separate bags, stored in the refrigerated shed, and then ground up together to create 'mink feed" The feed was fed through the grinder into a large tub on a wheeled cart with a tractor type seat for the driver.

A short distance from the grinding shed were seven very long open aired pens with metal "A" type roofs. Each structure housed hundreds of metal wire cages. Each cage was home to one or two mink. This time of year, it was breeding season so most cages held a male and a female mink for obvious reasons. As we headed over to the pens, my cousin was explaining the different attitudes and behaviors of mink to my husband. He told him that the mink were wild but passive most of the time, however they could be ferocious during mating season. He warned my husband sternly not to stick his fingers through the wire into the pens, he would get bit! So, on it went. We were educated on the many aspects of raising mink and the different processes which ultimately led to pelting season in December.

As we walked from pen to pen, my cousin and my husband moved on ahead of myself and my cousin's wife. I had been here many times before so I just let the guys do their thing. About halfway through the second run of cages, we heard a very loud yelp from my husband. He had ignored the warning and his temptation to touch a mink caused him to stick his finger through the wire and he got exactly what he was warned about. He still had his finger, but he was bleeding profusely. The tour came to an abrupt halt and we all returned to the house to tend to the bitten finger.

My Aunt and Uncle met us at the door, and as my sheepish husband walked past, my Uncle chided him saying that he had been warned not to put his finger through the wire! After a little first aide attention, my husband apologized for ignoring the warning and was forgiven. We would be returning to the farm many times over the years but he had learned his lesson and was never again tempted to put his fingers in the cages. **Lesson Learned!**

CIVVY STREET (House #2)

We had grown tired of living on the Base and decided to find a place in a nearby town, hopefully for a little less rent. Within a few weeks, we found a little bungalow on a quiet street and settled in for life on "civvy street". If you are in the Military, anything not owned or operated by the Military is considered civilian and any other place you live is on civvy street. It is a different life living on civvy street. People wear clothes other than uniforms! What a difference to see people every day in different clothes doing ordinary jobs, in ordinary places. It was a whole new world.

Let's Play Bridge

After we had moved into our new residence, we had gone to visit my parents on Friday night for an evening of card playing. My parents had played Bridge many years ago and I had always wanted to learn how to play. It turned out that while I was in Halifax during my time in the Navy, my husband had played Bridge with his friends on the Base. I was quite jealous that he knew how and I did not.

That evening while we were deciding which card game to play, I asked my parents if they would teach me how to play Bridge and they agreed. We would partner up, my husband and I against my parents. Bridge is a tough game to learn and has been known to cause trouble between partners who didn't always agree on which cards should be played. My parents were well aware of this possibility and my father made it perfectly clear that fighting between us as partners would not be tolerated.

It took me several Friday evenings to learn how to play the game. We never fought or even disagreed throughout this time. Eventually I understood the game enough and serious game playing started. We had a wonderful time at first, but we weren't long into the evening's game before the tide changed. I learned something that night that I had never known. My parents were fighting over the cards they were playing. I had never heard my parents even argue let alone actually raise their voices to one another. The arguing went on for about an hour. Finally, my father had had enough and stormed out of the living room and the game was over.

The rest of the evening was quite subdued. My father eventually joined us in the living room with a drink in his hand and quietly apologized for leaving the table abruptly. There was no explanation of the argument then, or forever after.

Fairly soon after his return, we said our good nights and left for home. My husband and I laughed all the way home. My father had thought that we would be the ones to fight and it turned out that my parents did all the fighting. He never apologized for the fighting, ever and we never played Bridge on Friday evenings again. **Lesson Learned!**

Get A Job – Doctor's Orders

We wanted to have children, but after four years of marriage, I was still not pregnant. We were getting concerned that maybe something wasn't quite right. I made a Doctor's appointment for a check-up. The results were all good. On a follow-up appointment, the Doctor asked me many questions about myself and my husband. His final advice was that maybe we were trying too hard. He suggested that I get myself a job and relax a little.

When I told my husband what the Doctor had said we agreed that I should look for a job nearby. I applied for several receptionist and book-keeping jobs in town. It wasn't long before I was employed by a newly formed construction company.

My new 9 to 5 job started right away. The office was only a few blocks from our house and I was able to walk to and from work. It was a small office on the second floor of an office building in a small strip mall. There were only two desks, a filing cabinet, and a telephone which sat on my desk. The windows in the office ran the length of the short south wall and faced onto the shopping mall. I was the only employee and all I had to do was answer the telephone, open the mail each day, and put it on my boss's desk. For doing these simple tasks I was paid very well, a lot more than I had expected.

As the days passed, I realized that I was going to be alone all day. My boss came in a checked his mail every two or three days, but the rest of the time I was alone. The telephone never rang. It was very boring. One morning when the boss arrived, I asked him if there was something else I could do to help. He said that the business was just getting started and it would be a while before there would actually be some work to do. He told me that he needed an office address and a telephone number to get started. He suggested that I should bring something to do to work with me, like a book or some knitting (knitting was the hobby that I had listed on my resume). I thanked him and he left.

I did bring a book to work, but I couldn't bring my knitting. My father had taught me that working in an office for someone was a responsibility and I should always respect the job I was given and maintain a business attitude. Knitting just didn't fit into that category. So, I spent my days looking out the window and reading some of the time. I was very well trained by my father's words and always felt guilty about even reading, but there was nothing else to do.

After a few months, we were heading into summer and the heat through the south window was becoming a concern. By the time August arrived, I had to do something. There were no curtains or blinds. The boredom had worn me down as well. When the boss arrived for one of his occasional visits, I told him that I was giving two weeks notice. He was disappointed but not surprised. I left my new job two weeks later.

And then I got sick. Off we went to my Doctor. I was pregnant! Checking my dates, we calculated that I had gotten pregnant two weeks after I started my job. The Doctor's advice to get a job had worked and broken the spell. My husband and I were ecstatic. The Doctor was happy for us and pleased that his advice had worked. I was due the following January. **Lesson Learned!**

A Grandfather's Wish & A Baby Bounty

About a year before I got pregnant, my whole family came together for a visit. There were my parents and my three sisters and their significant others. Ten of us in all. We partied-hearty (Navy expression), shared stories past and present, taking lots of pictures, as families do. One evening the conversation about the three past weddings brought us around to the last daughter who was going to be married the following year, they didn't have a date yet, though. The tone of the conversation changed a little when my father expressed concern that three of his four daughters were already married and he still had no grandchildren.

However, my father had an idea. He was going to put a "bounty" on babies. He offered $1000.00 for each baby born. My father liked to drink rye and seven-up when he partied, and other times too. He had four daughters and he wanted boys, so he told us he would add a bottle of rye for each boy. My father's sister and my mother were both redheads, so he added a bottle of seven-up for any redheads. He ended the offer with the statement that we should all 'get on with it'!

In the five years and 8 months that followed, he became a grandfather to eight boys and two girls. It cost him $10,000, eight bottles of Rye, and one bottle of seven-up for the first grandchild who was and still is a redhead! We often joked that he was presented with enough grandchildren to have his own Baseball Team. If he were alive today, he would also have 18 great grandchildren: 9 boys and 9 girls and I wonder if the Baby Bounty would still apply. I am certain that he would be thrilled even at the cost. His incentive worked and he got his grandchildren and his boys (he loved the girls, too), but a little bit faster than he expected. **Lesson Learned!**

A Look Into The Future

It is amazing how life goes around. We are retired now and living in the same town where our first son was born.

When we decided to retire, we discussed the many different options we had about where to live and what type of accommodation was available. One day while driving around, we decided to look for the little bungalow we had lived in when I first got pregnant.

As we drove up the street, we realized that the house was gone and they were building a large condominium on the area of the street where the bungalow used to be. We had never thought of living in a condo and knew nothing about condo living. We now had a new choice of accommodations as an option.

We spent a lot of time looking at different condos in the area. We even made offers on one or two that didn't work out. We finally settled on the condo where we currently live.

One Day while going through the information we were given when we purchased the condo, I ran across the name of the construction company and the owner who had built the condo where we now lived. Life had landed us in a condominium built by the company and the boss I worked for many years ago when I got pregnant - just because we had decided to look for the old bungalow. **Lesson Learned!**

THE FARMHOUSE (House #3)

As much as we liked the little bungalow, we now knew it was too small. Since I was out of work and pregnant, we decided to look for a new house to rent.

We found and rented an old farmhouse in the countryside close to the Base. It would be a much shorter drive to work for my husband and I would again be close to where my friends lived.

The landlord was a farmer with a large ranch a couple of miles away. He had some of his cattle grazing in the field behind the house and asked us to watch them for him. There was another smaller house across the driveway from us. A friendly couple lived there. We soon found out that they had a couple of goats. We found the house and the surroundings were interesting since we had never lived on or near a farm. We were not familiar with farm animals, and we looked forward to the experience. Something new to learn about.

Flies In The Attic

We had an extremely large front veranda with an entrance from the living room and a long stairway to the front lawn. Great for sitting out in the autumn evenings. The heating would be a challenge as the house was heated by two wood stoves, one in the kitchen and one in the living room. We figured we could handle it even though we had absolutely no experience with wood heat. The living room was quite large and ran the full length of the front of the house, as did the veranda. There was one large master bedroom and a tiny second room, big enough for our new baby. The kitchen wasn't large, but the counter ran down the side of the kitchen and would work well enough. At the end of the counter was a dining area and the doorway to the living room. Off of the kitchen was a long set of stairs down to the backyard with a pathway to the driveway.

The upstairs was one big attic. The first time we looked up there we were shocked with what we found. The attic floor was covered in about three inches of dead flies. There were some miscellaneous items left behind by previous tenants. Well, we would have some cleaning to do to get rid of all those flies. It took us a week of shoveling and sweeping to clean them out. A bit of an icky job but we soon got over it. If we were going to live in a farmhouse, on a farm, we would have to adjust to such things.

Over the next few years, we had to shovel out the flies every fall and sometimes in the spring. It was warm up there in the winter and there were vents at each end of the roof. The flies were here to stay. **Lesson Learned!**

Feeding The Cattle

In exchange for watching out for the cattle, the farmer brought us eggs every week. What a treat. We had never had farm fresh eggs before. We were amazed at how orangey the yolks were.

Eventually the farmer and my husband became good friends. The farmer would come every few days to bring feed and hay for his cattle. Since my husband enjoyed looking after the cattle, he asked the farmer if he would like him to do the feeding. The farmer readily agreed.

After a few weeks, the farmer showed up with six chickens, as well as our weekly supply of eggs. In his opinion, my husband was doing a lot more than was expected of him. The farmer was giving us our own chickens. There was an old shed a few steps from our backdoor, and the farmer and my husband set it up as a chicken coop. In addition to the coop and the chickens he was going to supply the feed as needed. The chickens and all their eggs were ours to keep.

My husband got into a routine of feeding the cattle, spreading out the feed and hay as instructed and gathering eggs and feeding the chickens every day. As the months of fall grew into the months of winter, it was a bit more work, but the farmer always came on the toughest days to lend a hand. He even came to plow the driveway when it snowed. Some days the work was a bit tough but we were grateful for all the help and the chickens and the eggs. What more could you ask for? **Lesson Learned!**

Pelting Season

On a mink farm such as my cousin had, winter was 'pelting season'. Mink farming was an acceptable profession at that time in our lives. We were interested in learning all about what was happening. We were invited to the farm on several occasions to learn what was going on. It was a wonderful experience for us. My father had been raised on mink farming in northern Alberta so it was especially of interest to me.

On one such visit in late November, before our son was born, my uncle asked us if we would like to help with the pelting. It would be hard work and long days during the coldest of weather in early December. We would work for about six days with a crew of other men and women starting at 8 am in the morning until about 6 pm in the evening. We would be paid for our work at the end of the pelting period. There would be a couple of short breaks and a lunch break. We thought it was a great idea and were anxious to know when we would start.

On the appointed day we were up early, had a quick breakfast, packed our lunches, and headed for the mink farm. My husband had applied for a week's holiday so our time was all ours. When we arrived, my husband went with my cousin to a different part of the system. He would be dealing with the big drums that the pelts were cleaned in, so I wouldn't see much of him until lunchtime. His job was to load the mink pelts into big drums that had a cleaner and sawdust that would clean the pelts and then transfer them to another drum to get the dust off and dry them out for fleshing.

My job would be different. I was assigned to the fleshing shed where the pelts were hung on hooks and the inside flesh was scraped off by hand. It was hard and tedious work, but I enjoyed it. The group I worked with were very friendly and we had a wonderful time. We told stories, and jokes and even sang songs. It may have been long tedious work, but the atmosphere, most of the time, was a lot of fun.

The first day was a steep learning curve and we were beat by the time the day was done and we headed home. The routine was the same for most of the week. At one point, there were some pelts that had tears in them. In the fleshing shed, we were given needles and thread to repair the tears. As it turned out, I was particularly good at sewing up the tears and I became officially appointed to repair all the tears we found. I would continue fleshing until someone had a tear and then I would mend the pelt. Some days all I did was mending. They were mostly small tears of an inch or two, but some were worse and took more time.

It was decent work and we thoroughly enjoyed ourselves. At the end of the day, we stunk! No shopping on the way home, no store would let you in. We drove straight home, changed, and washed our clothes, had a shower, usually had something to eat and went to bed. That was it for the whole week.

At the end of the week, payday, my Aunt and Uncle held a party for the whole crew and pelting season ended for us. We went home with healthy cheques, a bunch of new friends and Christmas spending money. We were almost sorry that the week was over, but then there was next year. We had not expected to work that hard, smell that bad, and have that much fun! **Lesson Learned!**

The Candles On The Piano

Long before pelting season, the weather turned cold so we flashed up the wood stoves in both the kitchen and living room. These two stoves supplied plenty of heat for us, the house was warm and cozy. It would cool off during the days of pelting but never got really cold. The landlord made certain that we never ran out of firewood.

As I planned Christmas decorations for our little farmhouse, I bought two candle stick holders for the top of the piano. Each candle stick held three decorated gold candles. They looked very festive and special. I was proud of the choice I had made and moved on to the rest of the decorating.

We put up a large tree because the roofs in the farmhouse were quite high. It was the biggest tree I ever had before or since. It was covered in lights and bulbs of all kinds. We hung lights outside along the roof of the veranda and the railing.

Now that pelting was over, we concentrated on Christmas presents. We had extra spending money for Christmas this year and spent a lot of time looking for unique gifts for both our families. We even bought extra nice wrapping paper. We were looking forward to the best Christmas ever.

In a few days it snowed and got colder. We had to flash up the wood stoves earlier in the morning and keep them fully stoked all day and into the night. We were warm enough and eventually the weather changed and we were able to use a little less heat.

However, there was an unexpected consequence to all that extra heat. In a day or two after the cold weather, I was devastated when I noticed that the candles on the piano had become too warm. All six of the beautiful candles had softened up from the heat and were now all flopped over like wilted flowers. They were a mess. They hadn't quite melted but they were so badly bent that I had no choice but to throw them out. I was so disappointed. There was no point in replacing them for the winter, they would just 'wilt' again. Candles would not grace my piano in the winter months again. **Lesson Learned!**

A Son Is Born

Our first son was born in late January, at 6:39 pm, the same time as the numbers on our current licence plate, and he was a problem right from the beginning. He was unable to get enough milk and was subsequently put on baby formula.

That's where the problem started. He was covered from head to toe in a red rash. Every ounce of milk he drank, came right back up. It was a harrowing experience for his new parents. He cried non-stop, all day and all night. We tried the different formulas recommended by the Doctor and suggestions from relatives and friends but he was not gaining any weight and was only five pounds, five ounces at two weeks old. Finally, my newborn son was hospitalized by the Doctor for tests.

Now I was crying all the time, too. To have a two-week-old baby in the hospital was devastating. They did not know what his problem was which did not improve our state of mind. We visited him a lot. In that time of our lives, Mothers and Fathers could not stay with their child and we were restricted as to how long we could stay.

One afternoon we arrived at the children's ward but could not find our son. Panic ensued! The nursing station reassured us that he was there and told us to re-check the room. Our son was not there or in any other bed in the room. The nurses now became concerned. They didn't know where he was either. The whole ward jumped into action, searching for our son. We had visions of someone else stealing our son. Where was he?

Finally, a nurse came into the room with our son in her arms. He was fine and sound asleep, something that was unusual for him. The nurse sheepishly explained. The beds had been stripped of their linens and replaced with fresh linen. There was an indentation in the middle of the mattress from constant use. Our son was so small, that while laying in the bed, his bedding covered him over and you couldn't tell there was a small baby in it. The laundry person had picked up the corners of the sheets and removed them from the bed to the top of her, now full, laundry cart. She then wheeled the cart to the laundry chute. Luckily, she had to return to the ward for more laundry before emptying the cart.

The nurse happened to pass her in the hall and asked about the laundry from our son's room. The two of them went to the chute and checked the cart. There, on the top, was our son, still wrapped in his bed sheets and sound asleep. It was a very scary story, but at the time we were just happy to have our son back safely. The laundry person was disciplined and the nursing staff were ordered to make certain that it didn't happen again.

Because our son was so small, we had a second scare a few days later while trying to visit him in the hospital. On arriving at his room, we could not find him again. Terror attacked our hearts. While my husband went for the nurse, I checked the middle of the crib, but this time he was not there. At the end of the crib was a "cuddle seat" and a small blanket. Before I had a chance to figure it out, the nurse arrived and lifted the blanket. There was my son, snuggled down into the bottom of the seat, sound asleep. Again, he was so small that you could not tell he was there. The nurse explained that after the previous scare, they were not allowed to leave him on the flat mattress in the crib, so they laid him in the cuddle seat for his own protection. **Lesson Learned!**

The Goat's Milk Cure

The Doctor had not solved the problem, but all the tests were negative. There was nothing physically wrong but he needed to gain weight. We were given a list of special formulas that would promote weight gain. We tried them all, but our son just spit them up. We felt that for every four ounces he drank, he would spit up five. And he cried all the time! Back then people would say that he had colic but the Doctor disagreed and felt that he had a low tolerance to the formulas. His only advice was to keep trying.

We had a habit of visiting my parents, sisters, and their husbands on Friday evenings. The first couple of weeks after our son was born, we still visited. When we arrived, my sisters and my mother would take my son for the evening, so that I could have a break. They were also concerned that he was not gaining weight as fast as he should and that he cried all the time. Looking back today, I suppose he was "lactose intolerant", but that was not common then. Everyone was convinced that it was colic and he would eventually grow out of it.

By the time he was three weeks old, we had tried everything that was suggested to us or ordered by the Doctor. At our recent visit, the Doctor said that we could try goat's milk, which was available in most stores.

As it turned out, we had a neighbour who milked a goat. We invited him and his wife for a visit. They were aware that we were having problems with our son. We approached them and asked if they could spare some milk for us to try. We could have all the milk our son needed but we didn't know if it would work. Within 24 hours, our son's rash was gone, he was keeping all the milk down and he slept! We were so excited. It was late

Saturday afternoon and we decided to go back to my parents to show off our new baby.

When we arrived with a quietly sleeping baby, my father could not believe it was the same child he had held the night before. His skin was clear of any rash and he woke up with his eyes wide and peaceful. We had a visit, marvelling in the change to our son. None of us could believe that a couple of bottles of goat's milk could make such a miraculous and rapid change. We all hoped that the problem was gone for good! Our son thrived on the goat's milk and gained lots of weight. He became so chubby that eventually we had to add skim milk to the goat's milk to stop him from gaining too much weight. We continued with the goat's milk and later that year we bought our own goat and with help from our neighbour we learned how to milk the goat and care for it. **Lesson Learned!**

Scrambled Eggs In The Barn

We were just beginning to learn about farming. We now had a dozen chickens and a goat and my husband was feeding a dozen or so cattle for our landlord. We enjoyed having our own eggs and milk, but it did take a lot of time, attention, and work. We loved it all, vowing to someday have a farm of our own.

One day we noticed that a few of the chickens were missing in the morning during egg collection. Later in the day all the hens were there for the head count, but our egg production was down. We wondered where they were at night. They weren't nesting, we knew because we didn't have a rooster and there were no nests in the coop. This absence continued so we decided to go on a quest. We went out each morning and counted the hens and were usually short about four hens. We also did a search in the evening when the count was again short. We didn't have any luck and no idea where they were going at night.

One morning, after my husband had gone to work, I went for a walk with my son, around the property. The weather had warmed up and spring was popping up everywhere, a good day for a stroll in the farmyard such as it was. The landlord had a large barn a short way out from the house we lived in and we strolled in that direction. I had never been inside the barn so I wanted to have a look. The landlord stored a lot of equipment and hay and feed in there. It was interesting to snoop around. I wandered into a section of the barn which was almost empty and I imagined that in the fall there would have been a lot of bailed hay in there.

As I moved around, I suddenly came across a lot of chicken droppings. Maybe our hens were spending the night in the barn. There were bits of feathers here and there, like there are in the chicken coop. I was now certain that the hens were here for the night. As I progressed, I noticed up ahead, what looked like splattered eggs on the floor. There were quite a few eggs here, but I didn't know why they were broken or where they had come from. The chickens wouldn't do that to their own eggs, maybe some type of animal was smashing them. I was sure that if another animal was messing them up, then they would likely have eaten them.

While I was just standing there, talking to my baby son about the problem with the eggs, I heard a noise above me and looked up. On the rafters, about twenty feet over my head, sat two chickens. The answer was quite obvious now. The chickens were spending the night in the rafters of the barn, then in the morning, they just sat there and laid their eggs which had nowhere to go but down to the floor below. Splat, scrambled eggs.

We knew what to do to keep them home. After work, my husband and I rounded up all the chickens and trimmed their wings so that they couldn't fly more than a couple of feet off the ground. The next morning, after the head count, all the chickens were there and the egg production numbers were back to normal. **Lesson Learned!**

However

In all the lessons we have ever learned, there is invariably a "however" somewhere that leads to the learning. In this case the 'lesson learned' came with a 'however' of its own. We had learned the lesson about why there were missing chickens at night and missing eggs in the morning. What we did not foresee, was the reason the chickens were in the rafters in the first place. Being novice farmers, we hadn't really thought this through.

Chickens living in a coop are not normally 'tree' dwellers and do not have a reason to spend their nights in the rafters. We hadn't thought about why they were there. We just clipped their wings to stop them from doing it and thought we had solved the problem.

It turned out that there was a particularly good reason and we were now paying a price for our smug 'problem solved' attitude. Our chickens were being attacked at night and very soon we had several dead chickens in the morning. They could not escape the predator because we had clipped their wings.

In the morning, there were feathers all over the place and chickens missing. We shored up the opening to the coop at night, but we then lost chickens during the day. We had no clue as to what type of predator we were facing. Eventually they were all gone. The farmer offered to bring us another dozen chickens and offered both sympathy and suggestions. So, we started again with a fresh dozen hens and some better protection. We did not clip the wings but we notified our neighbours and asked them to keep an eye out for what may be getting to our hens. The killing of the hens continued at a slow pace. We had built a fence around the coop for added protection, but the hens could still get out and therefore were getting attacked.

One afternoon, while my husband was in the field with the cattle, he heard squawking coming from the yard and saw another neighbour's dog and her puppy, running away with one of our chickens. He chased them through the yard, across the road and up to their driveway. We were furious that the other neighbour was not stopping his dog. He stood right there and laughed as his dog ran up his driveway with a chicken in its mouth. My husband hollered at him to keep his dogs away from the chickens, but he just turned around and went into his house.

The following day, the same scene repeated itself. This time my husband was inside and as he bolted from the house to chase the dogs, he grabbed his rifle with full intentions of shooting the dog. At the end of our driveway, the dog dropped the chicken, which was apparently unhurt as it ran back to the yard. My husband didn't stop there. He crossed the road chasing the dog and yelled at the owner. Once he had his attention, he told him that next time he would shoot the dog and the puppy. The neighbour seemed a little more attentive than last time. Later while talking about the incident, my husband was a bit worried that maybe the neighbour was concerned because he was carrying a rifle. Perhaps, he thought, it wasn't a smart idea to have yelled at the neighbour while he had the rifle in his hands.

As the days went on, it seemed that the dog attacks had stopped and our chickens were back laying eggs as normal. We decided that in the future, before we act, it might be better to think through the cause and effect of the resulting action, before it is implemented. In our attempt to keep the chickens on the ground and the eggs in the nests, we had stopped the ability of the chickens to protect themselves. **Lesson Learned!**

What Bathtub?

In December, it was pelting time again. My Aunt agreed to be the baby-sitter if I was willing to sew the torn pelts as I had done in the past. I agreed and so the week of pelting began.

During the week it started to snow heavily. Getting back and forth to the mink farm became a challenge for many of the workers and some days we were short handed. We had a Volkswagen and I had the best driver, so the trip to the farm was exciting to say the least.

As the last day of pelting drew to a close, we were in the middle of a blizzard. Several of the women were concerned about the drive home. My husband agreed to take an additional three people home. The trip took a long time. As can be expected the drive was treacherous and there were many vehicles stuck or in the ditch. We stopped to help out several drivers along the way. We managed to get everyone of our passengers home safely, but later than expected due to the challenging conditions.

We were happy to be on the last leg of our journey, almost home. The roadway on our street looked like it had not been plowed all day. We figured that if we didn't have to stop, we could make it up our driveway to the house. My husband had a method of hauling on the emergency brake at the last minute and then releasing it and turning at the same time which made the car slide into the turn without stopping. Then he hammered the gas and up the driveway we went.

However, this method, in deep snow and ice, made the car slide a little and by the time we got to the top of the driveway, the car had slid off the roadway and into the garden on the side. The car stopped with a thud. We had found a ditch of sorts in the garden. It was too late in the evening to worry about it. We got out of the car and into the house, where we stayed. My husband would deal with the car in the morning.

The next morning dawned bright and cold, but the snow had stopped. Fairly early in the morning the snowplow had been down the road which meant that the end of the driveway was deep in a roadway furrow but we weren't planning to go anywhere so it could wait. My husband bundled up, grabbed the shovel, and headed out to dig the car out of the garden. He was gone for quite awhile.

Eventually, cold and covered in snow, he came into the house. I had hot coffee and some cookies waiting. I did not expect the answer I got, when I asked how it went. He was laughing when he told me the car was still stuck, but that he had found 'the bathtub'. I was confused and asked him "what bathtub"? Where did the bathtub come from, what was he talking about? Apparently, sometime in the past, a renter had planted a bathtub in the garden. Over the years it became buried and overgrown and so we had no idea it was there.

When we drove off the driveway, the car slid sideways far enough to sink the front wheel over the rim of the bathtub and was now stuck inside the bathtub. We were going to need some help to get it out. We had spent several hours the night before driving carefully through many hazardous situations in the snow and ice, only to come home and get our car stuck in a bathtub! **Lesson Learned!**

An Invitation To Breakfast

My husband's time on the Base was ending. He would soon be posted to his next Destroyer and we would be moving back to the island. Our thoughts turned to where we would live once we got there. It was unlikely that we would find another farm like this. We definitely did not want to live in PMQs. We decided to try to buy a house somewhere quiet. Our funds were limited. We may have enough for a down payment on a small house, but it would have to be in a rural area, not the city in order for us to afford to buy. After some searching, we found a lovely place, in a small town. We now had a home to go to.

We would not be able to have a goat at our new residence, but we were informed that there were hobby farmers near town that had goats and it might be possible to buy goat's milk locally. Our neighbour here would buy our goat from us and we gave him the chickens.

Our farmer landlord was sorry to hear that we were leaving. We had become good friends. He had become dependent on my husband to care for his cattle. Good tenants and good help were hard to come by, he told us. He offered to help us if we needed any help to move. He told us how grateful he was for all we had done and then he invited us to a farewell breakfast with him and his wife and their two grown sons. Of course, we accepted. We knew his family and had met his wife and sons on several occasions. We looked forward to the invitation.

A few days before we left for the last time, we drove to his farm for a 10 am breakfast. In our world a 10 am breakfast was more like a brunch. In a farmer's world, it was breakfast. They started work on their farm at 5 am every morning when we were still sleeping. They worked for many hours before eating, so breakfast was at 10 am. We had a light breakfast at home that morning so that we would have a bit of an appetite left for the farmer's breakfast.

Breakfast for us was the bacon, eggs, and toast type of meal usually, so we just had toast that morning. We did not expect what we found before us in the farmer's kitchen. The kitchen was huge and the table was about eight feet long and four feet wide. It was enormous! The farmer's wife must also start to make breakfast at 5 am. This huge table was covered from one end to the other with more food than I had ever seen on one table. There was enough food there to feed my husband's entire Navy Base.

Soon after we arrived, the farmer and his sons came in, they washed up and then joined us at the table. There were greetings all around and then the plates were laid in front of us and we were invited to help ourselves. There were large plates of various kinds of sausages, all homemade. Bacon and ham produced from the pigs they raised and butchered. Lots of fresh eggs: boiled, scrambled, and fried. Several jars of home canned pickles, spreads, and jams. Mounds of home-grown potatoes and bowls full of every imaginable vegetable. And the amount of baking was amazing. His wife had fresh baked bread, buns, and sweets of all kinds. We wondered how we could possibly do the meal justice with our tiny little appetites. We were continually offered different servings of this and that. We ate for over an hour. The farmer's boys had huge appetites and the food on the table was greatly diminished by the time they were done.

I was curious and asked the wife if she did this every day or was it because they had company. I was assured that the men in the family went through this much food every day. What was left over was made into sandwiches for later in the field and some would be finished at dinner which would likely be a similar quantity. When they had family gatherings, the women would come the day before and they would cook all day for two days.

When it was time to say goodbyes and thank you, the farmer's wife had made up sandwiches for our dinner, packages of meats and baked goods for later. We took home as much food as we had eaten.

We had a great morning and a huge meal with the farmer and his family. We were going to miss them and our little bit of farming. Afterward, at home again, we talked about the breakfast we had and the enormous amount of food. We had no idea that a farmer's kitchen could produce that much food just for one meal. We knew that farmers were big eaters but never knew that they would eat that much food every day. I warned my husband that if we ever ended up with a hobby farm, he would never see that much food on our table. **Lesson Learned!**

Back To The Island

My son was now one year old and my husband was posted back to the island. We packed up our belongings and said farewell to our friends and neighbours. Our Volkswagen would not be able to pull the dune buggy, so my father offered to bring it to us once we were settled into "our new home". How nice that sounded!

PART 2

FROM THE PITCHING DECK OF A DESTROYER TO THE WHEEL OF A TAXICAB

The title of **PART 2** covers the story of our purchase of the town's existing bus company, thus chronicling our transition from Military life to Civilian life.

PART 2 is divided into two segments: the first relates to the lessons of our remaining time in the Military; the second segment is the beginning of the lessons learned during our Civilian life.

We were on our way back to the island with our new young son and a new car. Life was picking up. We had now bought a home in a small town on the island about a one hour drive to the Military base. No more Military housing or rentals. This was all ours! It would be a long drive to work each day and there would be other challenges because of the distance, but we would manage. My husband would often be back to sea on his Destroyer in the many months ahead. This would be our first real home and in a new town. A wonderful place to raise a family and learn new things.

FROM THE PITCHING DECK OF A DESTROYER... (1st Segment)

Don't Throw Out The Cat

Cats make wonderful pets. If you get them as kittens they can grow up with children and tolerate all kinds of little children abuses. Our cat was ideal and our son was taught to be kind to the cat, so they got along very well. The cat was litter trained and generally well behaved.

However, at some point after the cat reached adulthood, things changed. The cat was getting cranky. I can only assume that there had been some interaction between him and our son that had not gone well. Our son was just a year old at this point so anything was possible. The biggest problem was that the cat was now ignoring the litter box and messes were found in all manner of places. This was not good. Some places in the house began to smell. The living room was the worst. I was cleaning up messes as soon as I found them but I had had enough. No one wants a dirty cat, especially with small children in the house.

One cleaning day I found a mess behind the living room curtains. And then again, and again. When I walked into the living room one afternoon, I saw the cat come out from behind the curtains and I was furious. I grabbed the cat, yelling at it all the way to the front door. I opened the front door and tossed the cat out onto the front lawn with specific instructions to not bother coming back.

The cat landed on all four feet, as expected, and hit the ground running. He ran full speed across the lawn and right out onto the road in front of a heavy truck! He was killed instantly. I was upset of course, and full of guilt. I didn't want a dirty cat in the house, but I hadn't intended to kill the poor cat. Since then, I have never, and will never again, throw a cat out the door! **Lesson Learned!**

April Fools Day

Being a Navy wife is not easy and often lonely but as long as he comes home again life is good. After a couple of months at sea, my husband returned on March 31. My son and I were excited to see him drive into the driveway. The first day at home is always full of adjustments to our usual schedule without a man in the house. There are a million stories to tell on all sides. Tales from an eighteen-month-old are a little hard to understand but interesting, nevertheless. There are tales from the sea to tell and household problems to be discussed and planned for later.

By the end of the day, we were all weary from the excitement and were ready for bed. Bedtime routine changed a little of course but soon we were all sound asleep. We rose early because of the long drive to get back to the ship. After we said our goodbyes for the day, my son and I slipped back into our daily routine. Dad had his breakfast before he left, so I made breakfast for myself and my son, then we got dressed for the day.

As I sat down for my morning coffee, I noticed that Dad had taken the open pack of cigarettes from the table when he left. No matter, there was a full carton on the shelf over the kitchen sink. I reached for the carton, but it wasn't there. He wouldn't take a whole carton; he must have moved it for some reason. I looked around and couldn't see it anywhere. As I sat back down at the table, it dawned on me that it was April 1st, April Fools Day! He must have hidden it somewhere before he left. What a prankster! I scoured the house. I looked in every cupboard and every drawer and closet. I even went through everything in the garage and never found the carton of cigarettes. Surely, he would phone me in a couple of hours and say, "April Fools" and then tell me where he hid the carton.

It was now close to noon and no phone call. I would have to call him. It is not easy to call someone who is on board a Destroyer. You do not get a direct line to your loved one. It took about an hour to reach him. He was surprised to get a call from me and a bit alarmed that something was wrong. I reassured him that the only thing wrong was the missing carton of cigarettes and asked him where he had hidden the carton. He said he didn't know what I was talking about. My patience was gone by now. I wanted a cigarette and I wanted to know where they were, enough was enough. April Fools was over at noon, supposedly, and it was 1:00 in the afternoon. He promised that he had not done anything with the carton of cigarettes and didn't even think about it being April 1st until I told him. He had to get back to work, so we said goodbye, promising to figure it out later when he got home.

Now I was concerned. I was convinced that he had not hidden the carton of cigarettes, so what happened. I was taught to "walk backwards in my mind" when I had a problem like this to solve. So, I sat back down at the table and went back through the days and hours since I had bought the carton.

Nothing came to mind until I got to the night before. I remembered waking up during the night and hearing a cry from my son's room and then a thud. I had gone in to check on him but found him sound asleep and went back to bed. I was starting to think that maybe someone had broken in so I took a good look around. The top of the fridge was missing something and I quickly realized that our "change tin" was gone. There was not a lot in it, maybe $50.00, but enough. Then I panicked. My husband's month's pay was usually deposited to his bank automatically. However, on his return from this cruise, he had been given his month's pay in cash. He had given it to me the night before and I had put it in my purse. My purse was sitting right beside the carton of cigarettes on the shelf. I ran to the kitchen shelf; the purse was still there. I pulled it open frantically, afraid that the pay would be gone too. I couldn't believe that it was still there. How had they missed it. Better yet, how had they gotten in, my husband would have locked the door before he went to bed and there were no marks on the door.

I phoned the police to report the break in and the theft. There was little chance that we would recover the carton of cigarettes or the change tin but they would record the break in.

Later that evening, after my husband was home and I finally had a cigarette, we talked over the events of the night and the following day. It turned out that having been away for a while, he thought I would have locked the door. In my defence, I reminded him that, whenever he was at home, he always locked the door at night. Obviously, neither of us had locked the door! We agreed that our son's cry during the night must have scared off the thieves before they noticed my purse, and the noise I had heard must have been the door closing when they left. We agreed that from now on we would double check the locked door after he had been away and we promised never to play April Fool's Day jokes on each other. **Lesson Learned!**

Fresh Bread Is Meant To Be Eaten Warm

It was August and I was nine months pregnant with our second son. It was time to decorate the boy's room. We needed a new bed for the oldest son and dresser space for both. There was a full-length cupboard fashioned along the wall at one end of the room. We partitioned it off for two closets, one at each end and a 'change' table in the middle with shelves for baby stuff.

When I went into labour at the end of August, we had just started to paint the whole room. Dad was home for a few days so he carried on with the house chores and the painting. I would be in hospital for three days at least, as was the norm in those days. Dad decided he would bake bread in the morning, painting the bedroom in between the wait times. Our now almost two-year-old son was a great help I am sure and was dressed up in a long T shirt of his Dad's to help with the painting. Once the bread was baked, Dad set it on the counter to cool telling our son that they would have some for lunch after it cooled and then they went back to the painting.

At some point our son left the room and Dad went looking for him. He found him in the middle of the kitchen with a full loaf of warm, fresh bread in his hands, munching his way through the loaf. Dad took a picture of him standing there in his long 'painting shirt' with the half-eaten bread loaf in both hands, for posterity. When asked what he was doing, our son simply said that he was hungry and wanted some bread while it was still warm. **Lesson Learned!**

Christmas '74

After the birth of our second son, we were happily adjusting to the new schedule and adventures of having two boys. About the middle of November, the Navy decided to send Dad to Halifax for a one-year course. He had to report for duty January 4, 1975. We were all going to Halifax for the year.

We arranged to rent out the house while we were gone. Most of our furniture and belongings were packed and ready to ship to Halifax. Our new son's first Christmas would be a truly short Christmas. We wrapped presents Christmas Eve and put up the tree. After Santa came and Christmas day dawned, the boys had their Christmas. The older son was delighted with the wrappings and the toys but of course number two son was only 4 months old so not as enthusiastic. After the presents and breakfast, we took down the tree and boxed up the decorations.

The next morning, Boxing Day, we loaded up our car, packed up our two small boys, and drove east. We stopped in to see my folks on December 27, their anniversary, and introduce them to their new grandson. The following day we headed across country to Quebec to visit with Dad's folks who hadn't seen either of their grandsons. We arrived in Halifax on January 3, 1975. So much for settling in with our new schedule, but we did have an adventure. **Lesson Learned!**

Waiting For The Furniture

Our temporary accommodation, on arrival in Halifax, was a hotel room. When the Military posts you somewhere else, they cover all the expenses, including travel, furniture moving, accommodation and living expenses while you wait for housing. Most of this is very efficient, however, they cannot control the moving company. We had to stay in the hotel room for a month before our furniture arrived.

This might not sound too bad except I had two little boys to entertain in a small hotel room while Dad was away all day on his course. The baby did very well, but the oldest was turning two in a few days and the 'terrible twos' hit with a vengeance. Our son was a ball of fire. None of today's conveniences of 'all day kids TV' or iPads had been invented yet. We had some games, toys and colouring and drawing supplies but they didn't hold his interest for long. We often went for walks but this was Halifax, freezing weather, and lots of snow. The walks with a baby in a stroller and a toddler in hand were difficult and short.

Then came meals in the hotel restaurant. He was well behaved in the dining room but he just couldn't sit still, there was so much he wanted to see. He had his second birthday in the hotel dining room and they gave him sort of a birthday party including a hat and a cake. He also managed, while bouncing on the bed, to fall off the bed and hit his head on the end table, resulting in a nasty cut over his left eye which required a trip to the hospital and four stitches.

Finally, our furniture arrived and we moved into our appointed apartment for the year. We were grateful that all our expenses had been covered but waiting a month in a hotel for our furniture with two young children was exhausting and we hoped that we didn't ever have to do that again. **Lesson Learned!**

The Furniture

My parents had moved many times during my childhood, but I was unaware of any difficulties they may have encountered. We were inexperienced in moving so we relied on the good business practices of the movers. Most of our belongings arrived in good condition. Some items were missing; a couple of boxes of household effects and personal items which arrived eventually. Our sofa had a huge tear in the back and some parts to reassemble the recliner were missing.

The most important problem was the damage to our new Filter Queen vacuum cleaner. The vacuum was a round cannister which was hollow in the middle for the dust bag. The moving company had put a couple of heavy items inside the hollow for transport. The vacuum was about two months old and by 1975 standards, quite expensive. It appeared that the west coast packers were not aware of what can happen to plastic when it gets really cold. This furniture shipment, travelled across Canada and the mean temperatures of central Canada were well below freezing this time of year. The contents of the hollow vacuum cleaner had bounced around and literally smashed an integral part of the plastic motor casing and sub-sequently, a small part in the motor.

We did what we were supposed to do and forwarded a claim to the moving company which included pictures, descriptions, and receipts. We had signed an insurance agreement and paid for transportation insurance for our belongings. The Insurance company repaired the sofa and paid for the parts to put the recliner back together. They would not repair or replace the vacuum cleaner.

One of the reasons for our purchase of this particular vacuum cleaner, was its lightweight. We contacted the Filter Queen company to enquire about the cost of repairs. The vacuum motor and casing could not be repaired and a replacement motor would cost as much as the original vacuum product. Unfortunately for us, the Movers' insurance policy stated they only had to pay $.50 per pound on any household item and that included our lightweight vacuum cleaner. They sent us a cheque for about $20.00 to cover the loss of our vacuum cleaner. We never did replace the Filter Queen vacuum. **Lesson Learned!**

The Tree At The Fishing Hole

As Spring warmed the air and Summer approached, we started to explore the province we were living in. I had lived here many years ago and I knew the layout of the province. Still there was a lot to see. Dad and the boys had never been here before and many things had changed.

As we ventured out, I wanted to find the special places I had been as a child. The places I remembered most were the fishing spots my parents took us to for picnics and fishing. We were a family of four girls, but we all liked to fish, especially if we could catch something. There was a place called 'Grand Lake' where the fishing was great, unfortunately we could not find it on the map of the province and my memory was not good enough to find it so we decided on another spot on a river that ran through the province.

Not only were we able to find the river, but the spot on the riverbank where my family used to fish was still the same. A few weeks later we decided to go camping at this spot. We packed everything we needed, including a playpen, into our Volkswagen and drove to the riverbank. We pitched our tent up close to the sandy bank under a large old tree and set out the playpen for our youngest. That tree was probably there when I was a young girl. We sat with the boys and fished a while but didn't catch anything. The boys played in the sand and had a wonderful time. We organized the tent for the night, putting the playpen inside for the boys' sleeping quarters and settled in. The boys were asleep in minutes, they played hard and were tired. We talked awhile and then fell asleep too.

Several hours later, we were awakened by a very loud thunderstorm. The tree was sheltering us from most of the rain but the lightening and the wind started to concern us. The boys slept through the entire event. Dad and I got scared. We were afraid that the tree might fall on us in the wind or lightening might strike it and knock it down. Our fears got the best of us and we were now terrified and probably irrational.

Picking up the boys, we left the tent and went to the car. We spent the rest of the night curled up in the car. In the morning, the sun was shining and the tree was still standing. We had breakfast, packed up and headed home. We talked about our fear of the tree coming down. It turned out that neither of us enjoyed high winds and trees in the first place.

We returned to the fishing hole a few weeks later. Since we had last been there the tree had fallen down over the bank with its top resting in the river, and the large trunk lay across the sand right where we had pitched our tent. We had been lucky not to be there when it actually fell. We never went back there to tent again. The fact that the tree actually fell, along with the wind and lightening that we didn't like, has stuck with us ever since. **Lesson Learned!**

Military Transportation Home

Late in the year we received a letter from the agent managing the renting of our house. The renters had to leave before we returned at the end of January and had decided to move at the end of November. The house would be empty for two months. We decided that I should take the boys and go home in December. Dad would get alternate accommodations on the Base. We made all the arrangements for the move and booked a Military flight as far as Trenton, Ontario. Then I would fly to Winnipeg for a visit with my sister and her family. Later a stop to see my parents and then home.

I landed on the Military Base for the night and had a commercial flight to Winnipeg scheduled for the next day. The Military will fly family members who are returning home anytime and we thought this was great. No one told us that this was not the way to fly with young children. We were told that there would be accommodations on the Base for myself and the boys to stay overnight. Sure enough, we were assigned a room for the night, with cribs for the boys.

However, the quarters were two blocks away from where we and our luggage were off-loaded. This was an airport for Military personnel and was not set up to handle moms and their children. There were no taxi cabs available on Base. There were no carts to move luggage, or kids, around. I had three pieces of luggage and two toddlers to take to our room on the second floor, with no elevator either. We ended up making three trips in the freezing cold at 10 pm at night. I picked up one piece of luggage at a time, carried the youngest boy in my arms and had the oldest "help" me carry the suitcase. We would rest a few minutes to warm up when we got to the room and then head back and repeat the procedure until we were done. The boys were tired and cranky of course and so was I. It was a trying experience.

Finally, we were done and I put the boys to bed after a drink and snacks that I had with me. It turns out that the only food available on the Base was a canteen several more blocks away and it closed at 8 pm. Fortunately I had packed some snacks and drinks so we had enough for breakfast in the morning.

I was exhausted but before going to bed myself, I checked my luggage for clean clothes in the morning. I was extremely disappointed to find that the carton of cigarettes I had brought with me and my hair dryer were missing. Someone had stolen them from our luggage while we were trudging back and forth to our room. One would think that our luggage would be safe on a Military Base. Not so! This method of transportation had been an unbelievably bad idea. **Lesson Learned!**

A Short Visit In Winnipeg

We managed to arrange for a taxi in the morning to take us to the airport. The boys and me had slept well and were refreshed. We had time before our flight for a quick breakfast at the civilian airport and then on to Winnipeg.

My sister and her husband met us and we travelled to their home. By the time we arrived it was the middle of the afternoon. We were all tired and needed a nap. Something was wrong because I was not feeling well. After a short nap with the boys, I knew I was sick. The boys were fine and happy as ever. We were to stay here until we could book a flight home but I had to go to the airport to make the reservations. I was not really in good enough shape to do that but there was no choice.

My sister minded the boys and my brother-in-law drove me to the airport and stayed with me while I arranged a flight for the next day which was earlier than I had originally planned. I was too sick to stay longer. The 'all too short' visit in Winnipeg had not been worth the trouble we had gone through. I was happy to be heading home. Obviously, I had paid an unexpected price for the night in Trenton. **Lesson Learned!**

Home Sick

I spent an uncomfortable night at my parent's house. By now I was running a fever and coughing a lot. My mother offered to drive us home and stay a day or two to help me unpack. The movers were to arrive at 10 am the next morning, so we had to leave early.

When we arrived, the movers informed me that they had been there waiting since 8 am and they would not unload the truck until I paid them $80.00 for waiting two hours for us. I didn't have $80.00 in cash and they would not take a cheque. My mother reluctantly paid them in cash and insisted on a receipt.

As soon as they had unloaded, I curled up on the sofa with a blanket and slept. I left my mother and the boys to fend for themselves. We had brought some groceries with us so they were fed and napped when I finally woke up. I was now sicker than before and needed to see a doctor, but I didn't want my mother to have to stay too long. After a couple of days of unpacking, I told her I would be fine and she could leave. She knew I wasn't well but not how sick I really was, so she packed up and left.

I called a babysitter and took a taxi to the Doctor's office. I had a high fever and a bad case of Strep Throat. When I got home, the babysitter said I looked awful and to go to bed. She told me she would stay a few hours, take care of the boys, and do some unpacking. I was incredibly grateful.

The Doctor called the next day. He had done some blood tests when I was in his office and the results were in. Not only did I have Strep Throat but I was also about four months pregnant! I had been so sick that I hadn't even suspected that. When Dad called to check on me that evening, he got a pleasant surprise. I was home again and in my own bed with a bunch of antibiotics and four months pregnant, but this was not the home coming that we had planned. **Lesson Learned!**

A True Friend

The next day the babysitter returned for a couple of hours to help with the boys and the unpacking. I received a phone call from one of the friends we had met in Halifax. He was now out of the Navy and had arrived on the west coast. He wondered if he could come for a visit. I told him I was too sick for company, but he insisted on coming to help out.

When he arrived the next morning, he sent me to bed and told me to stay there. He was going to take care of everything. He literally took over. He fed the boys, cleaned the house, got groceries, and finished the unpacking. He also made certain that I had everything I needed including getting my prescription refilled. I spent an entire week in bed.

As I improved, he let me take over what ever I could manage and he maintained the rest. I was feeling much better and Dad was due home in a few days. Our friend insisted on staying until Dad was home. I had never had such care and was forever grateful for his care and attention to our boys while helping me through the worst days of my life. He never asked anything in return. A devoted friend. **Lesson Learned!**

Grocery Shopping Trouble

Dad returned from Halifax at the end of January and everything returned to normal. Almost. When we left for Halifax the year before I had a son heading for the terrible twos and a four-month-old baby, but now I had two active toddlers and I was pregnant again.

Dad went off to work every day and I needed to get back to a normal routine. The boys were fairly good but continually active. The oldest was an adventurer and took his brother, now almost two, with him everywhere. They were usually playing in the backyard but tended to wander a little, so I needed to keep a close eye on them.

We only owned one car which was normal back then, so the boys and I would walk the short distance to town and back for groceries. As they grew used to the trip and the shopping, they got a little braver and started throwing tantrums in the store. I had a tough time getting groceries and overseeing them at the same time and we still had the walk home ahead of us. One day I just parked the cart at the front of the store and told the clerk I would be back in a couple of hours to pay for the groceries. We had an unpleasant walk home.

When Dad got home, I sent him to the store to pick up the cart of groceries I had left behind. Later we talked about this problem because he would be leaving for three-months on the Destroyer and would not be around for grocery pickup. We had no solution.

By the time I needed more groceries he was gone. I had thought about the problem and had an idea. When the boys and I got to the store, I told them that if they were good in the store, we would go to the restaurant for French fries when we were finished shopping. They behaved like angels!

I got all the groceries and off we went for French fries. I wondered if this would work every time, and it did. For the next three months of Dad's absence, grocery shopping became a treat for them and a pleasure for me. **Lesson Learned!**

The 'Buy Me Bug"

As our kids grew older the shopping experience changed and the treats were no longer necessary to keep them calm. Once our daughter was born, she learned her behavior from the boys and was never a 'problem shopper.'

However, all three developed a new issue of wanting everything they saw in the store. They pretty much knew they couldn't have the things they wanted but they would nag me anyway. Three young toddlers nagging the whole time became a bad habit that needed a solution.

Together, Dad and I decided to try a new tactic. Every time they asked for something, we would tease them that they were being bit by the "buy me bug." They very soon caught on to this little quip and started teasing each other and the problem was solved. They no longer wanted to be the one to be bit by the 'buy me bug' and no matter where we were or what store we shopped in the same principle applied.

To this day they still use the phrase and have taught their own children to beware of the 'buy me bug'. **Lesson Learned!**

Snake & Monsters

The kids' Dad always had an enthusiastic sense of humour which occasionally caused some interesting reactions. As they grew up, they learned to develop their own sense of humour as a result. This was a good thing. But while they were little they did not always know when he was teasing.

Dad and I had gone for groceries one afternoon while they were in school. They were still quite young and in elementary school. After school, the boys in particular, were always hungry and knowing that we had been for groceries, they headed for the fridge. The youngest son spotted a garlic sausage coil. They had never seen one before, so he cautiously asked his Dad what it was.

The sense of humour came to the surface as Dad explained that it was a 'snake'. He got the reaction he was expecting as our son slammed the fridge door and jumped back. At first he thought it was a live 'snake' and needed some reassurance that it was dead. The oldest son was curious as to what all the noise was about and came running. The youngest was still quite disturbed and told him there was a snake in the fridge! Of course, he had to see for himself, and his reaction was pretty much the same as his brother's. He slammed the fridge door in fright and backed across the kitchen away from the fridge.

Dad was howling with laughter and I was frantically trying to calm the boys down. Finally, they settled down and I made their father explain what was actually in the package they had seen and then he had to prove it. We cut open the garlic sausage and cut up some muenster cheese, put some crackers on a plate and with some reluctance the kids tried the 'snake'.

However, we normally bought cheddar cheese so there were cautious questions about the new kind of cheese on the plate. I assured them it was just a different type of cheese called "muenster" cheese. They accepted the explanation and enjoyed the snack. Over the next couple of weeks, we ate all the garlic sausage and the cheese. As time passed the boys wanted more but never said anything.

When we took our kids grocery shopping next time, we had only been in the store long enough to start our shopping when the oldest hollered across the store to his Dad, asking if we could buy some 'snake' and 'monsters'. First of all, he obviously meant muenster cheese but he mispronounced it in little kids' language and he was not quiet about it. What the whole store heard was two little boys, begging their Dad to buy snake and monsters!

We lived in a small town and knew most of the people in the store, so it took a while to explain to the other shoppers what it was that the boys really wanted. This scene repeated itself many times over the years and to this day, one of the kids' favorite snacks is still referred to as "snake and monsters". I eventually forgave their father for the embarrassment that I endured in the grocery store for years because of his teasing. **Lesson Learned!**

A Pile Of Groceries

While the kids were young, there were many times when they had to learn new behaviors and as parents, we had to learn along with them. They were definitely more creative than we were. Once such incident came the day after a Saturday shopping trip which included a large load of monthly groceries.

In our small kitchen, the larger, heavier items like bags of sugar and flour were stored below the kitchen counter. They were too heavy or bulky to go into the smaller cupboards above. When the kids were little, it wasn't customary practice to lock things up and even electrical sockets were not covered in those days. In the lower cupboards in my kitchen, in addition to the obvious bags of sugar and flour, were boxes of noodles, rice, spaghetti, breakfast cereal, a bag of dried peas, a bag of oatmeal and even a box of cookies. All of these were newly bought and unopened.

As parents, we did like most adults and slept in a little on Sunday morning. Our young children, on the other hand, usually were up and about before we were. Most days they just played while we slept. This Sunday was one to remember. When we walked into the kitchen for our morning coffee, we were met by three little rascals and a huge pile of miscellaneous groceries.

Attempting to get themselves some breakfast, they had gone through the bottom cupboard looking for something to eat. However, they had done a lot more than just pulling everything out of the cupboard, they had opened and emptied every bag and box. In the middle of the kitchen floor was a huge pile of groceries. Everything had been dumped out of their containers; all mixed together were flour, sugar, broken spaghetti, dried peas, oatmeal, all of it. The only box they hadn't managed to open was the box of cookies, which they were working on when we arrived.

There would be no way to salvage the groceries we had bought. They had spent a lot of time playing in the pile as they added to it, and everything was thoroughly mixed! Asking them what they were doing just met with the fact that they were hungry and were looking for the cookies. There was a great deal of scolding that followed and I am sure that they were sent to their rooms to think about it while we cleaned up the entire kitchen floor.

We learned three things that morning: one was that we needed to give up the practice of sleeping in on Sunday mornings; the second was that the kids should not be left alone if they are likely to be hungry; and third, that we needed to lock up the groceries in the bottom cupboards. The one thing that puzzled me, was how they managed to open all those boxes and bags that I usually had to struggle to get open, even on a good day! **Lesson Learned!**

The Missing Soothers

Before our second son was born, we got a puppy and named her Velvet. She was a small terrier and became a great friend to our sons. Our oldest was still attached to his soother. To be honest, I was relying on the soother to keep him happy. We soon learned to have spares around so that when he lost one, there was always one to replace it to avoid tantrums. When son number two arrived, we needed even more soothers.

After a couple of months, it became apparent that we were going through quite a few soothers that we never found. We suspected that our oldest son was losing them out in the yard or flushing them down the toilet. One day as I walked through the living room, where our two-month-old son was laying on a blanket, there was the dog, laying right beside him with one of the soothers in her mouth. We have pictures!

Well, that explained why the boys were always losing their soothers but we still never found all the missing soothers. We wondered where they were. While watching our oldest playing with the dog in the backyard on a sunny afternoon, I noticed that he had given Velvet his soother. It dawned on me that maybe the dog was the culprit, abetted by our son. On a whim, I took a walk around the back yard and found what could be freshly dug holes.

I got an old spoon from the kitchen and used it as I dug into the ground and found a very well chewed and dirty soother. The dog was guilty of soother theft and was burying the evidence. We decided the best way to save on soothers would be to pin them to the boys' clothes so they could not give them to the dog or leave them somewhere for the dog to steal. The dog still occasionally got caught with a soother in her mouth but the number of thefts, and holes in the yard, decreased significantly. **Lesson Learned!**

Visiting The Mayor

Our oldest son was our biggest education during his early years. Dad was on a Destroyer at sea many weeks, and even months, at a time. I had a challenging time keeping my eyes on all three young children. The boys tended to wander off occasionally. Our local area was a small town, so they didn't often go too far. Mostly they wandered down the street and back, but there was a river nearby so it was always concerning when they disappeared.

The oldest son was always adventurous and there were afternoons of frustration and worry when they were gone too long. Our friends and neighbours knew them well and were a major help in locating them and bringing them home. They were like a couple of puppy dogs that wouldn't stay in the yard and had to be rounded up and brought home regularly. One afternoon after they had been gone a little too long, there was a knock on the door and my neighbour was there with the two boys in tow.

She told me she had received a call from the Mayor's wife. Apparently, the Mayor and his wife had been out shopping. When they came home, they found the boys sitting on the sofa in their living room watching TV. The Mayor's wife had explained that she didn't recognize the boys and the boys said that they didn't know where they lived. She had called our neighbour to see if she knew who they were and she was certain she did.

The Mayor's wife was a little miffed that the boys were in her house but admitted that she hadn't locked the door when they left. She gave them each a cookie and sent them home with our neighbour. Of all the places in our small town that the boys chose to invade, they had to pick the Mayor's house. Very embarrassing. I immediately phoned the Mayor's wife and apologised profusely, promising that it would never happen again. The very next day, I wrote our name and phone number on the inside of the collars of all the boys' jackets and told them it was there in case they got lost again. I also explained in 'kid speak' not to go into anyone else's home and what would happen to them if they ever did it again. **Lesson Learned!**

Who Is Dana?

At about ages 3 and 2, we had a great backyard and a sand box for the boys to play in. Our next-door neighbour had two young boys of similar age as well. The four boys played to together for hours every day. None of the boys was old enough to talk very well and were still talking in small phrases. They were able to understand each other somehow, but hard for parents to understand sometimes.

My daughter was still a baby, so I used to sit with her on the deck and watch the boys play, occasionally supplying cookies and drinks. One afternoon, while listening to the chatter amongst them, I heard one of the neighbour boys talking to 'Dana'. I wondered who he was addressing. It was not the name of either of our boys. Then I heard my youngest son address his brother as 'Dana'. 'Dana' was not his brothers name either. I thought maybe I had heard them wrong and went about the rest of my day.

After a few days, I heard the youngest referring to his brother as 'Dana' again. I took the youngest aside and asked him why he called his brother 'Dana'. He said that was his brother's name. I told him what his brother's name was and he disagreed. I asked him what his name was and he knew that, so I let the subject go and thought maybe talking to my next-door neighbour might shed some light on the issue.

She knew both the boys' names, but she noticed that her sons were calling our youngest 'Dana' because they thought that was his name. I asked her if they knew the oldest son's name and she said that they definitely did. So, why was there a problem with the youngest's name. As it turned out, they had never heard the name before so they just picked something they knew that was similar and easy. So, if they were actually referring to the youngest son, why was he calling his brother 'Dana'?

He was only two years old, but he knew his name. The neighbour boys were talking to 'Dana' and as it turned out, our youngest son had assumed that since that wasn't his name they must be talking to his brother, so he called him 'Dana'. Even after trying to convince him that 'Dana' was not his brother's name, he continued to call him 'Dana' instead of his real name.

When he turned five and started kindergarten, he was still calling his brother 'Dana' and for several years after. The oldest son never seemed to mind and eventually just considered it a nickname. **Lesson Learned!**

The Master Of Escape!

Number one son was a handful. Always active and curious. I never knew what to expect next. With three toddlers now, we built a five-foot-high fence around the yard intended to keep them safe from wandering. The fence was built of cedar boards placed vertically and close together and the gate was always locked to keep the kids inside. In spite of this, number one son managed to climb up and over the fence. The problem was the drop to the ground on the other side. To this day, I have no idea how he managed to work his way up and over the fence.

That day I was busy doing 'house things' and did not know he had left the backyard. There was a banging on the front door and when I opened the door, there stood my son, his face covered in blood. It was a very scary sight for any mother. After cleaning the blood from his face and trying to calm him down, I found a nasty cut above is left eye and knew that he needed stitches. Dad took our car to work and the hospital was a half-hour's drive away. I called the Fire Chief, who happened to be a neighbour and who was home for the day. He agreed to drive us to the hospital and his wife would look after the other two kids. Our son got three stitches that day.

After an inspection of the other side of the fence, it was obvious that we would have to convince the next-door neighbour to clean up his side of the fence. He had tossed a bunch of vehicle parts and oil cans up against the fence. Our son had picked the worst possible spot to land. There was nothing we could do to the fence to stop him climbing it again, it was already high enough. The only thing we could do would be to convince him not to do it again.

He had not enjoyed going to the hospital for stitches and we hoped that the experience would be enough of a teacher, along with a good scolding it seemed to work. However, his wandering days did not end because he did learn how to open the gate no matter how we locked it up. Although he became our household's "Master of Escape", he never climbed over the fence again. **Lesson Learned!**

Early Morning Rescue

Our oldest son did not only escape from the backyard he also went out the front door once he was tall enough to reach the doorknob. There are many ways to lock a door these days that are available, but back then solutions were limited. We only had one lock and it was on the outside to keep others from getting in. We needed a way to keep him from getting out.

His favorite destination was his grandparent's house across town and he knew how to get there. He would encourage his brother to go with him and off they would go early in the morning before we were up. They would take their tricycles and peddle across the bridge that spanned a narrow part of the river and up the street to Grampa's house. When they got there, Gramma would make them breakfast and then phone us that they were safe and we would drive over to bring them home. We suggested that maybe she should stop making them breakfast and send them home to discourage their adventures. Grammas don't do that so the treks continued.

Finally, we put a hook and latch on the very top of the door to prevent it from opening. One morning our little "Master of Escape" used our broom handle to lift the latch and they were off to Grampa's house. Unfortunately, this particular morning, Gramma and Grampa were still in bed and did not answer the door. The boys banged harder on the door and still no answer. Next, they had found Grampa's shovel in the garage and luckily, just as they were about to break the glass window in the door, Grampa opened it.

Later, our son told us that they thought Grampa must be hurt and they were going to help. After this harrowing experience, the grandparents decided that the boys' adventures were not quite so cute. The grandparents were proud that the boys had tried to save them but they agreed that it was time to make them stop. They took our advice. They scolded the boys and told them not to come to the house early in the morning or without their parents. **Lesson Learned!**

Every Parent's Worst Nightmare

It was the Christmas season, so we put the kids into the car and travelled to another town with a large department store to shop for presents. It was pouring rain and fairly late in the day when we arrived. The store would be closing in a little more than an hour, but we still had time to shop.

Taking the boys by the hand and our daughter in a stroller, off we went. Our first stop was the toy department. We didn't plan to buy toys with the kids in tow, but they were excited and needed something of interest to them. After the toy department, we went to the clothing department. The kids were growing and needed some new winter clothes. We let them help pick out jackets and mittens. Our oldest son picked out a bright yellow jacket, an excellent choice for our wanderer. The other son was having trouble deciding what he wanted so I focused on him. Dad and the other two were headed to the girls' section.

A couple of minutes later my son made his choice and we were off to join the others. When we caught up to them, the oldest son was not around. We couldn't find him and started to get concerned. Dad and I split up, each taking one child with us. We scoured the store, asking everyone if they had seen him. No one had seen him. We checked the boys' department and the toy department. At one point, I left the younger son with his father and went out to the car. It was dark now and still pouring rain. He was not at the car and I noticed that there were only a few cars left in the parking lot. I was terrified that maybe he had been kidnapped! I returned to the store just as they were announcing that the store would be closing in ten minutes. We had just enough time to search the store once more.

We walked around a corner and there he was. He was sitting on the floor against a wall crying but safe. I picked him up and hugged him tight and calmed him down.

He explained that he had stopped to look at some decorations and couldn't find us afterwards. While he was looking for us he ran into a Santa and asked him to help him find his Mom and Dad. Santa told him to go away, the store was closing and he was going home. He broke into tears again saying that Santa was mean to him. Later when everything settled down, I tried to explain that the Santa he saw was not a real Santa just a mean man dressed as Santa and that the real Santa was a nice man. Dad and I were extremely disappointed that a Santa had treated him so badly and hoped the experience didn't affect how he would feel about Santa in the future. It didn't. He loved all the other Santas he met along the way. However, the whole incident stayed in his parent's memories a lot longer. **Lesson Learned!**

Robbed Again!

When our daughter was a few months old, we went second-hand shopping one Saturday afternoon. We found a wonderful, large wicker chair with a side pocket for only $5.00. It was a great find. We could put it on our front porch and I could sit out there while feeding my daughter. I loved it and after we brought it home, I spent a few days cleaning it up and painting it a pale mauve. It looked beautiful and was just a perfect size for the porch. It was wonderfully comfortable and my daughter and I spent many days sitting there watching the boys play as the summer went by.

As my daughter grew older, the chair became used less often. One late fall afternoon, the weather was unusually warm, so I made myself a coffee and took the kids outside to sit in the afternoon sun. When I opened the door, I was shocked and disappointed. The chair was gone. It was obviously stolen but we weren't sure when. It had been several days since we had been on the porch, but it was there the last time we were out. We couldn't imagine someone stealing it. It was only worth a few dollars and it was so large it would take a pickup truck to take it away. Nevertheless, it was gone.

In hindsight we probably should have chained it to the railing. We reported the theft to the police but it was unlikely that we would ever see it again, but because of the size, style and colour, someone might find it. I was sad that I hadn't taken a picture of it. Our family is all grown now with families of their own, but I have never stopped looking for it or one like it. I really loved that chair and the memories that come because of it. **Lesson Learned!**

Who Is That Man

There are turning points in every stage of life.

Dad had been away now for three months. The three kids were still toddlers. There had been many cruises for Dad since they were born but they were still young and less able to understand who was supposed to be there. His coming and going was just as much a part of their lives as friends coming and going.

As they learned to talk, they called him Daddy when he was there but weren't old enough to know who he was or why he was gone. I was so excited that he was coming home. He had been gone for an eternity it seemed. I missed him so much I could hardly wait. While he was "at sea" there were only letters, no phone calls. It was very lonely.

I told the kids that Daddy was coming home, but they didn't really understand. He had been gone so long they had forgotten all about him. When he walked through the front door, I was there to greet him, but the kids hung back a little wondering what all the fuss was about. When I calmed down a little, our oldest son looked up at me and asked me who that man was. The whole atmosphere changed. Dad was devastated. I realized that the kids didn't recognize him. I told them it was Daddy and their demeanor changed immediately. They knew what Daddy meant. I had told them often enough but they only recognized the word not the man.

The confusion only lasted a minute or two then they ran up to greet him. The second oldest son was shy and it took him a little while to react. Dad and I talked later. He was quite upset that the kids would ask who he was. It was probably a turning point for him that influenced his future decisions. **Lesson Learned!**

...TO THE WHEEL OF A TAXICAB (2nd Segment)

Due to a series of unfortunate events, the Military was no longer what Dad wanted to spend his life doing. He wanted out. On the 10th anniversary of his enlistment, he applied for a release. He shopped around for trades in electronics but they didn't suit him. Locally, a taxi and bus company was available for sale which interested both of us. So, along with raising three toddlers we decided to become entrepreneurs.

While visiting my parents during our transition from Military to business, my husband asked my Dad what he thought about our new venture. He told my husband that 'he thought he was crazy but he admired his guts'. My Dad thought we were 'crazy' on several occasions in our life.

Pneumonia

D ad was quite ill on one of his trips and ended up with pneumonia. On board ship the attendants in the "Sick Bay" did not believe it was that serious and did little to treat him. When he arrived home, he felt a little better being off the ship. He called his superior and requested three days of sick leave. The Captain of the ship was not happy with him being away. Also, he was scheduled for a "Fire Leaders" course in a few days and was told that he was expected to be there regardless of how sick he thought he was.

Dad was furious. The "Fire Leaders" course meant that he would be up to his chest in icy, cold water most of the day. Not a smart idea for someone with pneumonia! A few nights later he woke up in a cold sweat and was having trouble breathing. His only solution was to drive to the Navy Hospital an hour away. Once there, they took x-rays and he saw a doctor who confirmed that he did indeed have pneumonia. He was given medication and sent home for a week. He was told not to take the "Fire Leaders" course.

He got over the pneumonia in a few weeks and resumed work. He found out that the Captain was quite angry with him after receiving the Doctor's report and the time off for recovery. He was an integral part of the communications team on the ship and he wanted him there.

Our agreement to purchase our new enterprise was due to be finalized December 15. Dad was supposed to be released from the Navy well before that. We had made many plans in preparation and had received the necessary financing. We were good to go. We had even hired our friend from the Navy, who the kids now referred to as "Uncle". Unfortunately, the Captain, continually delayed the paperwork required for Dad's release. Finally, the Captain said that he lost the paperwork and had no intention of granting the release in any case. We had thought that acquiring Dad's release was just a matter of paperwork, easy. **Lesson Learned!**

Due Diligence

You can't just walk away from the Military. If you try, they will lock you up in jail, in Dad's case that meant Edmonton, Alberta. He had to go to work and our friend and I would have to run the business until we could force the Captain to file the paperwork. Unhappily, Dad went back to work.

My father was a Military man and had taught me many things. I knew what I had to do. I had to make a case for the fact that a young mother with three young children could not run a business alone. I made a Doctor's appointment to discuss my health in the face of the situation. The Doctor agreed that it was not a good idea to do this alone. I asked for a letter to that effect which I could submit to the Captain. He did better, he actually spoke with a Military physician who had a serious conversation with the Captain on my behalf. The Captain wouldn't budge but the seeds were planted. I wasn't done yet.

I went to the Minister of my church and explained my predicament and concern for the well being of my children. He immediately agreed and had an associate on the Naval Base with whom he was willing to discuss the situation. As it turned out he was talking about the head Chaplin on the Base and he also had a few choice words with the Captain who was more reluctant than ever to give in. Dad's Divisional Officer came to him saying that he shouldn't make any more trouble, and Dad agreed.

I had one last thing I could do. The Military has a Family Welfare Office, so I called. Dad's Divisional Officer heard what I had done. He chastised Dad reminding him that that they made a deal about no more trouble. Dad told him that he had made the deal with him, not his wife and she could do whatever she wanted.

Family Welfare Office was concerned enough to suggest sending an agent to meet with me, I agreed. By this time, we were a couple of months into running our business and Mondays in the taxi and bus world were generally quiet. It was the weekends that were wild. I suggested he come on Monday. Just as the sun came up Monday morning, everything that could happen or go wrong did. It was the worst day I had ever had since we started the business and even one of the boys was sick, throwing up regularly. The agent arrived in the middle of a household and business disaster.

Nevertheless, we had a lengthy conversation about the Captain's position and Dad's desire to leave the Military. I didn't have to say much, he could see what was happening. He went back to the Base and his report was not what the Captain wanted to hear. However, Dad got no indication that he would change his mind. His Destroyer was due to sail in a few days, and he wanted Dad on that ship! Dad would be sailing on Sunday morning and there was nothing he could do.

Unintentionally, I got really sick. Friday I had a very sore back and by Saturday morning all I could do was cry. I was crying, it seemed for no reason. Dad got really concerned. He thought I was having a nervous breakdown because he was sailing the next day. He drove me to the hospital and within a few hours they had taken my temperature and blood tests confirmed that I had a severe kidney infection and I would be spending over a week in hospital recovering.

Dad phoned his Divisional Officer and told him that he would not be on the ship in the morning. But he wasn't out of the Navy yet. The Captain had been warned! I had done my 'due diligence'. **Lesson Learned!**

Just One Phone Call

That afternoon while I was in hospital, Dad was at home tending to his kids and running a taxi business with the help of our babysitter and Uncle. He decided it was his turn to make a phone call. He did me one better, he called the Prime Minister in Ottawa. Unfortunately, he was told, the Prime Minister was currently out of the country, so he called our Federal Member of Parliament. After a conversation with him, the MP asked Dad to give him a few days to look into it and he would call back.

When he called back a few days later, he told Dad he had good news and bad news'. The good news was that as of that moment he was officially out of the Navy and the bad news was that he would have to go back to work for a day, when the ship returned, to do the paperwork. Dad was in awe that the MP could work so fast. The MP said that I had done the right things and the Captain had no right to keep a man in the Navy while his family was suffering, especially after all the information I had provided.

The MP had initiated a "Ministerial Inquiry" and all the people I had talked to had also done their due diligence and there was a ton of paperwork to back up Dad's claims. 'Just one phone call' had brought it all together and the Captain had no choice but to release him. **Lesson Learned!**

Nowhere To Hide The Spray Paint

Now, we were a full fledged, Taxi and Bus Company, operating 7 days a week, 24 hours a day. Dad, I, and 'Uncle' each had our roles to play. Raising the kids and maintaining some normalcy in their lives was my main job and my secondary job was accounting for everything – business and personal. I was busy. We had added a small desk at the end of the kitchen to put the telephone and answering machine on for Taxi calls. The kids learned that they were not to play with anything on the desk and they didn't.

For some reason we had purchased a can of red spray paint and it was stored in the garage on a shelf. It took no time at all before the oldest found it. He didn't know what it was or what it was for, he couldn't even read at this age. I took it away from him right away and moved it to a different shelf when he wasn't around. A couple of weeks later, he found it again. He seemed fascinated with the can for some reason. If I had been a bit smarter or maybe not so busy I might have gotten rid of it right then. However, he didn't know how it worked so I didn't think any more about it and I asked Dad to put it on the top of the kitchen cupboards where it would be out of sight and well out of his reach.

One early morning when the oldest was the first family member up and around, as he usually was, he spotted the can of red spray paint on top of the kitchen cupboard and he went for it!

He opened the bottom cupboard drawer to use as a step and climbed onto the counter. We aren't sure how he reached the top of the cupboard, but we assumed that he used the cupboard shelves as steps. Nonetheless he reached up and took down the spray can. Some how he figured out how it worked and had a ball spraying the kitchen floor, cupboards, the entire front of the desk and then headed for the laundry room where he spray-painted the washer, dryer, and the hot water tank. When I woke up, he was in our bedroom, spraying the bottom corner of the blanket on the end of our bed! I had spent days making that blanket but I kept it for many years anyway, red paint and all.

We realized that the only way to stop him would be to get rid of any spray cans we had. We had a tough time cleaning the kitchen and the appliances. We repainted the desk, because we couldn't get all the paint off of it, and also painted the hot water tank. The kitchen floor was sculptured tile and that took months of continual scrubbing to clean up. As you may imagine, our son has never heard the end of our frustration that day. We learned the hard way that there is nowhere to hide spray paint from an active, curious child. **Lesson Learned!**

"JungleGym For Active Children"

About this time, Dad's parents had moved to town to be near their grandchildren. They decided, without talking to us, that our active boys needed a **"JungleGym For Active Children"** swing set to play on. They ordered a set that was eight feet high. It was built as a triangle and was eight feet on each side. We had a large yard so the size was not a problem. It had swings and hand rings hanging from the top and a ladder for climbing. Great fun for our oldest son, not so much for our younger, less adventurous son. Our daughter enjoyed being pushed on the swing but was far too young to do anything else. We thought it just might be a good thing to keep our curious son busy. We were right, it did keep him busy, he spent most of his days playing on it and I could watch him from the kitchen window. At least I knew where he was.

One morning while doing the laundry, our youngest son came running in to say that his brother needed help getting off the swing. Sure, enough there he was dangling down with one foot stuck in one of the two rings. I don't know how he got himself in that position in the first place but he definitely needed help to get down. He was quite happy and unhurt. I told him not to do that again.

Another day I looked out the window and saw him sitting eight feet in the air on one of the corner cross supports. I was concerned that he might fall and wandered out quietly so that I didn't startle him and asked him nicely to please come down. He wiggled a little this way and that and then slid down one of the poles. I thought to myself that I didn't need to worry, he seemed to know exactly what he was doing. I warned him to be careful and went back to the house.

After a few such occurrences, I actually stopped worrying about him. Then came the really scary part. I looked out my window and there he was walking along the metal pipe frame at the very top, in bare feet, eight feet off of the ground. The steel pipe was only about 2 inches in diameter and he was walking around all three sides with perfect balance – so far! I was terrified that he was going to fall. I was afraid to go outside and tell him to get down. He might get startled and loose his balance so I just stood at the window and watched him. Eventually he stopped, bent over, and slid down one of the poles. Later I talked to him about it and asked him not to do that again because if he fell he could get badly hurt. He promised no more walking on the top.

When we finally moved to another home, the **"JungleGym"** stayed behind because our new yard was too small, thankfully. The **"JungleGym For Active Children"** was definitely as advertised and definitely a lot more dangerous. **Lesson Learned!**

Mother Nature's Plumber

Our daughter was walking now and starting to be as curious as her older brother. Her curiosity was gentler than her brother's and she had a unique perspective. She only got into things she could reach, like the soap in the bathroom which she promptly flushed down the toilet. The soap was a new bar and naturally plugged up the toilet which subsequently flooded the bathroom. Minor stuff like that. The soap was a small bar and we easily unplugged the toilet. Problem solved. The toilet became a focal point for her and she loved to watch the water swirl. She was still quite young and scolding her didn't always solve the problem. I tried to keep her busy with the other toys she had.

We had bought her one of those ring toys where the colourful plastic rings have a hole in the middle and the kids put them on a stick with the largest one on the bottom, then four the smaller ones all the way up. The largest one was about three inches in diameter and I imagine it was great fun to watch it swirl as it went down the toilet. Another plugged toilet and lots of water.

We plunged that toilet a dozen times and it seemed that we managed to move the ring around a bit but the toilet never flushed like it should have. We didn't call a plumber because the toilet did flush but it took a noticeably longer time to drain.

Many months later our area had a small earthquake. The next morning when the toilet was flushed, it was back to normal. The earthquake had shaken the house just enough to loosen the ring and flush it away. Mother Nature's plumber had done the job! **Lesson Learned!**

The Penny

O ur daughter's constant curiosity varied from unimportant things to greater problems. The worst was her need to open anything she could find. Drawers were fascinating. Kitchen drawers, dresser drawers, bathroom drawers were all subjects of her curiosity. It was hard to keep ahead of her investigations and remove anything she might get hurt by or damage. Eventually they were all made safe and I worried less.

I shouldn't have stopped there. She found a new fascination with the heat registers in the floor, which I had never checked. Some of them were dusty and had cat hair in them which I should have paid more attention to in my housecleaning efforts. The dirt and dust weren't much of a problem for her, but one register near the kitchen had a trove of small bits and pieces of toys that proved to become a major disaster. She found that register and managed to get the cover off of it and salvage its contents which included a penny. For some unknown reason, she put the penny in her mouth and then swallowed it. All of a sudden she was coughing violently and crying. It was difficult to understand her problem, since she didn't know how to tell me what was wrong. I was now starting to panic because she was having trouble breathing. I called to Dad and we were off to the hospital in minutes.

It seemed that it took forever to get there. A nurse asked what happened and I explained as much as I knew, stating that she had managed to pull something out of the heat register and put it in her mouth. I did not know what she had swallowed. They immediately took her away for an x-ray. Waiting was excruciating. Finally, a Doctor came and explained that our daughter had swallowed a penny and it was, at this time, stuck at an angle, vertically in her throat. He informed us that she would have to stay in the hospital overnight. They were going to feed her "cotton batten and peanut butter" sandwiches to try to move it through to her stomach.

They would take x-rays again in a few hours to see if there was any improvement. If the penny didn't move down her throat on its own, they would have to operate to remove it. They assured us that the sandwiches should help move it down.

We spent a long night waiting for the news. No parent wants an operation on their child. In the morning, the Doctor confirmed that the penny had been dislodged and was now in her stomach. She could go home. However, we were to watch her carefully until she passed the penny naturally. If she had any problems, she would have to return for more x-rays.

In a couple of days, the penny was out and life returned to normal, almost. Dad went through the house and attached all the furnace vents securely to the floor in a way that enabled me to clean them out more often but would prevent our daughter from opening them in the future. We all had quite a scare and didn't want to ever have a repeat. **Lesson Learned!**

On Santa's Knee

Our new business also included providing freight pickup and delivery to stores and businesses in town. Preparing for our first Christmas as a business, Dad decided that he wanted to wear a Santa suit to do his deliveries and pickups. We went shopping for a Santa suit. Explaining to our young children what he was going to do, was not possible, so he left the suit at the office and would change in and out of it there. We also purchased a bag of candy canes for him to hand out whenever he ran into children on his rounds. He wanted to play the role well so he behaved just as Santa would whenever he was in the suit.

As word got around that he had a Santa suit, the local photographer asked if he would sit for pictures with the local children before Christmas so that they could have a photo with Santa. He agreed and on Saturdays before Christmas the photographer offered "pictures with Santa". It was a great hit, just about every child in town had their picture taken. The photographer offered to take a picture of Santa with his own children if Dad thought that would work. We agreed. We have several really beautiful photos of our three children with Santa that year. They were so excited that they never even noticed that it was their Dad.

He became known as the town's "official" Santa which endeared him to the businesses he serviced for years, an unintentional benefit of being Santa. **Lesson Learned!**

New House, New Car

We were offered a large contract with a transport company from the nearby city. We bought a Hino, a straight bodied 10-ton truck. Now our driveway was too small. A personal car, two taxis, a panel truck and a small bus all left no room for a big Hino. It was time to move, again.

We found what we needed just outside town and we sold our modest first home to Dad's parents who had always loved the house and yard.

Dad's parents, particularly his Father, were not impressed with us for running a business of our own. He didn't think we would ever make any money and were wasting our time. Even as time went on and we succeeded in our venture, he would never admit that we were "successful". As he explained to us, no one he had ever known was successful, therefore, since he knew us, we couldn't possibly be successful. It was an irrational statement at best. Unfortunately, he had a bitter life growing up, and was deeply affected by the stock market crash in the thirties but we had come to understand his strange ways. Dad was quite deflated by his father's attitude. It meant a lot to him to have his Father's approval. However, our business was doing very well and we considered our venture a success in spite of his opinion.

Our Accountant said that we needed some deductions because we were making too much money. He suggested that we buy a new car. So, we bought a new car, a very flashy car, a black Buick with a gold vinyl top. It was a Buick Le Sabre two door turbo coupe with lots of room for the kids. It looked wonderful. Dad was so proud of his new "wheels". He couldn't wait to show his father. Surely now he would accept that his son was a successful businessman.

We all proudly climbed into our new car and drove over to Gramma and Grampa's house to show him our beautiful new car. When they came out of the house, Grampa walked slowly around the car, then turned to his son and told him that he would never have a two-door car even if you paid him. Then he walked back into the house. That was all he ever said about the car or anything else that his son did. Dad was dumb-founded and very saddened, but he realized later that there was nothing he could do to ever change his father's mind. **Lesson Learned!**

The New Sofa

We had a new home but it was an older house and needed some minor repairs and renos. We also needed some newer furniture. We bought a new kitchen dining set and still think it was the best piece of furniture we ever bought; it was perfect. Now we needed a new sofa. We took our time looking. We had children to get settled and an expanded business to run. Shopping for a sofa was far down the list of things to do. Eventually, we found the sofa we wanted. We had our own truck, so it didn't have to be delivered.

Like I said, this was an old house. When we got the sofa home, we quickly realized that we had a big problem. The front of the house had only one window and one doorway. Both were too small for the sofa. We could not get it in through the narrow doorway. As well the window was obviously too small. We had planned to take out part of the living room wall at the front of the house to get more daylight, but that was a future venture. We should have either made it a priority or postponed the sofa.

However, for some reason, when the house was built, the largest window on the main floor was facing the neighbour's house. Luckily, it would be big enough to get the sofa through – maybe! The window was also about six feet off the ground. It was a logistical nightmare. Dad rounded up three strong friends and they went at it. They had to take the frame apart but managed to feed the sofa in through the window finally. And it rained the whole time! It took a couple of days to put the window back together and for the sofa to dry out. No harm was done and the window was repaired and better than it had been. Next time we would measure everything, not just pianos and sofas, before we purchased big items. **Lesson Learned!**

A Winter Without Glass Doors

We only had one door to the house, which was not safe. In case of a fire, we only had one way out. We also had no deck to sit on. We decided to add a deck to the front of the house and included sliding glass doors into the living room: an after-thought considering the problem we had moving in the sofa and the lack of exits. It was a job that would be too much for us to do on our own given the time it would take. We found a local handyman who said he would be willing to do the job. At that time, no one in our town had a large deck, just patios at ground level.

Our house was built on a slope, with a steep driveway down to the road. The deck would need to be about four feet above the ground at the foundation and would run the full length of the front of the house, about thirty feet long and would be fifteen feet wide. We also wanted a roof over the deck, the full length. We were going to have double sliding glass doors installed into the living room wall. It was going to cost a lot but our builder offered us a great deal.

We planned to start in late October and the job would be done before it got too cold. This was important because the opening for the sliding doors would have to be done first. We hung heavy plastic over the opening while we awaited the arrival of the doors. The deck was a thing of beauty, the first in our area. The deck itself was finished well ahead of schedule. We were able to get all the finishing touches and painting done before the weather got too cold.

However, (there is always a "however") the sliding glass doors had not arrived. It was bad enough that the living room had a gaping hole in it, which we covered with heavy plastic, but the contractor would not answer his phone. Eventually we got a message from him saying that the windows had been delayed and we would just have to be patient. We were quite frustrated at the turn of events since he had already been paid and we were concerned that there maybe a chance that he was skipping out of the job. We hassled him by phone constantly. Occasionally he would respond with some other excuse, but no doors were forth coming.

We had several snowstorms to contend with and a unique 'open air Christmas'. Finally, the weather warmed and our lives improved but still no doors. We thought that perhaps he had underbid the job and subsequently ran out of money. He probably did order the doors and then couldn't pay for them. Finally, we got a call from him and he was going to bring and install the doors about four months later. The deck was great when it was completed. Our whole family made terrific use of the space and spent many hours visiting and barbecuing with friends. After spending most of the winter without windows, in the future we would do renovations during warmer weather and with more reliable trades' persons. **Lesson Learned!**

The Kids' Movie

In the days before the internet, we only had one small TV with limited service and only one or two channels. Watching TV with the kids meant making sacrifices on both sides. However, as parents you tend to save your programs until the kids have gone to bed. They would have priority over the TV during the day, even on weekends. Both Dad and I liked to watch Canadian hockey games in the fall. Luckily, most of the games were on Monday nights and that fit well with the kids schedule since most of the suitable shows for them were on during the day.

Unfortunately for us, and for them, one year the Stanley Cup games were going to be held mostly in the late afternoons on the weekend. There was a lot of complaining from the kids about having to sit through hours of hockey. During one particular week, the TV advertised a movie that the kids really wanted to see and it was cancelled because it was supposed to be on at the same time as one of the final hockey games.

Dad was determined to watch the hockey game and the kids were upset. Finally, a day or so before the weekend, in a moment of frustration, Dad told the kids that he would phone the TV station and tell them to move the hockey game to another day so that his kids could watch the movie.

Later that night when the kids were in bed, I asked him what he was going to do when the hockey game was on instead of the movie. He just sighed and said that he would just have to tell them it didn't work. The next afternoon, while watching TV just before the hockey game, the announcer related that there had been a problem and the hockey game was postponed to the next day, and then the movie started. The kids were amazed and excited that their Dad had convinced the TV station to move the hockey game to another day just for them. He became a hero to his kids and all their friends. Of course, he never made the phone call but we never told the kids. Sometimes things are simply better left unsaid. **Lesson Learned!**

Dog In – Cat Out

Eventually, after moving in was all settled, we ended up with a cat. A well-trained cat this time. It started out as a kitten and the kids had to learn how to treat her. As she grew they learned what she liked and didn't like. The cat was trained to use kitty litter and learned to hide when she had had enough of the kids. She would curl up with them on the sofa and sleep in their beds with them at night. She became a well loved and accepted part of the family. Later on, the kids pretty much ignored her most of the time and became busy with other things in their life.

Then they decided that they wanted a dog. Boys always want a dog; girls are typically happy with a cat. Dad was on their side so we would get a dog. We all piled into the car and went to the city pound to buy a dog. Dad and the kids fell in love with one particular dog named Clyde. Not a little puppy but a year-old German Shepherd cross, an almost full-grown dog, full of energy. We stopped at the pet store and bought dog food, a dog dish, leash, collar, the whole works. We never gave a thought to whether the cat would like the idea, after all our other cats had gotten along with the dogs we had.

By the time we arrived home the kids and the dog, all in the back seat, were well acquainted and having a wonderful time. Even Clyde seemed to be enjoying the ride and all the attention from his new-found family. As I carried our new purchases into the house, the kids and Clyde bounded into the living room, which as other cat owners know, had now become the property of the household cat. The invasion was not well tolerated. In less than a minute, the cat fled out the living room window. Clyde had not chased the cat, she had just decided on her own that she didn't want to be there, so she left. We all expected that she would return when she was ready. The kids loved the dog, but they missed their cat, especially our daughter. Sadly, the cat never returned and we never even saw her again. The dog came in and the cat went out! **Lesson Learned!**

The First Fish

We decided it would be fun to take the kids fishing for the first time. We had some fishing gear but needed to buy some children-sized fishing rods. We bought some new gear and one small fishing rod. We lived near a river known for good fishing and wouldn't have to go far. There were a couple of flat areas that would be safe for the kids to stand close to the water and fish.

Off we went. The kids were all excited. We had packed some snacks and lawn chairs. It took a while to rig up the rods and Dad took his time explaining the process and various parts to his young sons. I was not too certain that they understood much of what he said, but he was teaching his "boys" how to fish. My daughter and I sat back and played in the sand.

Eventually, the rods were ready and the lines were in the water. The oldest son had Dad's old rod and the younger one had the new, smaller rod. The water in this part of the river was shallow and slow moving, so Dad had put bobbers on both lines so that the boys could tell when they got a nibble. There was a lot of excitement several times when a bobber popped under the water.

So far neither son was catching any fish but they were having a lot of fun. All of a sudden, there was a squeal of delight from the youngest as his bobber disappeared beneath the surface and didn't pop up right away. It re-surfaced for a couple of seconds and then disappeared again. This time the rod almost bent in half. Our youngest son was terrified by the pulling on his rod, dropped the rod and ran away from the shore, screaming. Dad was right there beside him at the time. He quickly grabbed the rod before it got pulled into the water.

After I calmed our son, he started to take an interest in what was happening. He gradually moved closer to where his Dad was standing with his rod. Soon, the fish was under control and ready to be reeled in. Dad told his son to come and help him land the fish. He told him it was his fish and he should help. Together, each with their hands on the fishing rod, they reeled in and landed a 3lb rainbow trout.

Even as adult fisher persons, we never caught a fish that size. Pictures were taken of course. The fish our son had caught was almost as long as he was tall. No wonder it scared him. By the end of the day, he became immensely proud of the "Big First Fish" he caught! **Lesson Learned!**

The Dog & The Bear

Once a week was garbage day. It was Dad's job to put the black bag full of garbage out at the end of our somewhat long sloping driveway. He usually did that early in the morning before going to work. In the late fall, after the time-change, it was dark at this hour. Our dog, Clyde was used to the routine and would accompany Dad with enthusiasm. He often stayed outside for awhile after Dad returned to the house.

On one such morning, in late fall, he started barking loudly. It was unusual behavior for him. Dad went outside to see what all the fuss was about. There, halfway down the driveway was a big black bear. Clyde was frantically, bouncing up and down barking at the bear. He was getting a lot closer to the bear than Dad thought was safe, so he called him back. Clyde was so absorbed in the bear that he wasn't listening. Dad hollered at him and finally got him to come back. At the sound of Dad bellowing, the bear ran across the lawn and down the road and was soon out of sight.

We wondered what had brought the bear so close to the house. It was unlikely that it was the garbage because it wasn't a garbage day and our garbage had never been touched. Then it dawned on us that we had an apple tree in the front yard. It was fall and apples were on the ground rotting. A great invitation to any bear. We spent the better part of the day, cleaning up all the apples.

Later in the week, it was garbage day and Dad put the garbage out as usual. Soon after he returned to the house, Clyde started barking again. We became alarmed thinking that the bear was back. Returning to the driveway, Dad found Clyde halfway down, barking at the end of the driveway where the garbage bag was. Clyde thought that the big black garbage bag was a big black bear! Dad all but dragged him back into the house. We were all relieved and Clyde had calmed down.

It didn't end there. The next week, on garbage day, Clyde started barking again at the black garbage bag. We guessed that this was going to happen every week until we found a way to stop him from thinking it was a bear. The best solution was to put the garbage in a garbage can. We bought a silver, metal garbage can to put the black bag into. Problem solved and we also learned to keep the apples off of the ground in the fall. **Lesson Learned!**

The Freight Protector

C lyde loved to ride in the front seat of Dad's Hino while he delivered freight. It became his habit that after his morning rounds outside, he would station himself beside the passenger door of the truck to wait for Dad. He often sat there for half an hour patiently waiting until Dad arrived, checked over the truck and then let him into the passenger seat. Off they would go together for the day. Dad would give him a break about lunchtime, but otherwise, he just sat in his seat, enjoying the ride.

Occasionally, he would lie down for a nap, with his head in Dad's lap. He was a full-grown shepherd and too big to stretch out in the seat. Like all dogs he often stuck his head out of the window to enjoy the breeze, especially when the weather was warm. They travelled all over the area, picking up and dropping off freight of all sizes, from small automotive parts to complete sides of beef. He never left the truck during the stops but closely monitored Dad's comings and goings.

On one such trip, a worker walked up to the window to greet the big shepherd in the truck. Clyde obviously decided that he was a little to close to the truck in his care. Although he could have made a lunge for the worker because the window was all the way down, instead he just growled threateningly. The worker was startled and backed away abruptly. Dad was nearby and immediately walked quickly to the truck to find out what was happening. He had never heard Clyde growl or threaten anyone. He was concerned that Clyde might jump through the window and attack the worker. This was a new development.

Clyde was always gentle when other people wanted to talk to him or pat him, his behaviour was concerning. Clyde did not attempt to leave the truck but continued to growl until he saw Dad approaching. Dad walked up to the window, gave him a pat on the head and told him he was 'a good dog'. Clyde returned to his usual position in his seat and stopped growling immediately. Dad advised the worker that the dog was not aggressive but he obviously did not want anyone too close to the truck when Dad was not near it. During future deliveries to this establishment, Dad was told that word got around, not to mess with the Hino because there was a big dog protecting it. **Lesson Learned!**

School Bus Naps

When our oldest son started Grade 1 it was a milestone as it is in any family. It took some getting used to. We had to be ready earlier in the morning for the School Bus. He was gone all day and the second oldest son was not used to being without him around. His personality changed as well as his interests without his brother to guide him and talk him into all sorts of trouble.

Later in the day, the bus would drop him off and we would all sit and have snacks and listen to the events of his day and tell him of ours. As the novelty of starting school wore off, we slipped into a different routine and life went on as normal.

Occasionally, I heard tales of the oldest falling asleep on the bus ride home in the afternoon. He was getting a good night's sleep so there was no reason for concern. It was a half-hour ride and he was the last stop of the afternoon for the bus. He just played hard and was tired, so he fell asleep.

One afternoon, he did not come through the door at the appointed time. I thought maybe the bus was late. After a while, I started to get concerned. Had something happened to the bus? I phoned the school but no one answered. The school was closed for the day. I phoned his teacher at home and asked her why my son had not come home. She had no idea. She was certain that he had gotten on the bus and the bus was on time. She suggested that I call the Superintendent and gave me the phone number.

I called, a little frantic now, and there was no answer but I left an extremely nervous mother's message and hung up. Dad wasn't due home for a couple of hours. I phoned a couple of other parents to see if their children were home. All were accounted for, so where was my son? In a short while the Superintendent returned my call. He said that the bus was parked in the bus yard as usual and the driver had gone home.

I expressed a great deal of concern that my son was not home. I asked him to call the driver and find out where my son was. He said he would do that and called me right back in a matter of minutes. He had located the driver who said he didn't remember when my son got off the bus and then realized that he hadn't stopped at our house. When he got near, he had looked in his mirror and didn't see him so he kept on going, thinking that he probably hadn't been at school that day.

The Superintendent assured him that our son had been to school that day and had confirmed with his teacher that he had gotten on the bus. The resulting conversation with the bus driver revealed that he hadn't actually checked the bus when he parked it. The Superintendent and the bus driver met at the bus yard and opened the bus. There, in a seat near the back of the bus, was my son, still sound asleep. He was curled up on the seat and not visible from the front of the bus.

The rather sheepish bus driver knocked on my door with my son in tow. He apologized profusely. I thanked him for bringing him home. He promised that he would pay special attention to his sleeping passenger in the future. **Lesson Learned!**

Auction Rabbits

After we had settled into our new home and our business was progressing well we decided to buy some rabbits. We studied how to build rabbit cages and raise rabbits for food. Eventually we reached the point of going to the livestock auction nearby. It was an interesting experience for us. We had never been to an auction before. We learned the lingo and the how-to methods. We also found a ready supply of rabbits for sale. The prices were quite low, the younger rabbits were the highest price because they were the best eating. Older rabbits were quite a bit less.

When we arrived home, we decided to convert our garage into a small barn in which to build rabbit cages. Following a day at the hardware store, we began construction on a row of rabbit cages. We bought bedding for the cages, feed for the rabbits and were off to the auction to get some "fryers" as the young rabbits were referred to.

At the auction, we picked up our bidding card and sat down to watch the sale. There were lots of rabbits being sold. We waited a while, letting the prices go down a little and then bid on a few lots and ended our afternoon with four fryers. We remained there for a while longer to see the rest of the rabbits sold. When they got to the larger, older rabbits, the prices dropped steadily. In the end we bought a large buck for about $2.00 and thought we had made a great deal.

We did not butcher the rabbits right away. We had read that livestock of all kinds can often be given a shot of antibiotics to "perk" them up for auction and that the best thing was to wait a couple of weeks for the shots to wear off. We don't know if this was the case with the rabbits we had purchased but felt it was better safe than sorry, so we waited.

Two weeks later, we set about butchering a couple of the young fryers. We had butchered deer in the past, so we were confident that we could handle rabbits. It was not difficult and in a short time the rabbits were ready for the roasting pan. Dad and I had warned our children that the rabbits were intended for the table. We instigated a rule in the house that was maintained as long as we had livestock. We did not allow the kids to give the rabbits names. We told them that in the future we would buy them a rabbit as a pet and they could give it a name, but any rabbit meant for dinner was not allowed a name. Young as they were, they seemed to understand and never gave names to the livestock that was destined to the table. **Lesson Learned!**

Tough Rabbits

We all thoroughly enjoyed the young rabbits that we had bought at the auction. Now came the day to butcher the large buck. He was no more difficult than the younger ones, but his hide was thicker, and I decided that eventually I would try my hand at tanning some rabbit hides.

Cooking the older rabbit was a different matter. I prepared it the same as I had the younger fryers. That's where things changed. We now knew why they were not selling well at the auction. They were really tough. Not a very enjoyable meal, but still edible. In any case, we thought the big, older rabbits were definitely a good buy and I wanted more hides to tan.

We made several more trips on Saturdays to the auction and bought more fryers but were reluctant to buy the older ones. We also often stopped for supplies at the hardware store on the way home. While wandering through the store we noticed a meat grinder and once we were home we discussed the possibility of grinding the older rabbits into ground meat to make them easier to eat. It sounded like a great solution. Next weekend we were going to buy a meat grinder and some larger rabbits at an auction price that was hard to refuse. **Lesson Learned!**

Bunny Burger!

uying more big rabbits at the auction was easy. They were not a popular item for the sale. There were a few buyers, but not a lot of interest. We easily picked up three larger rabbits under $5.00 each. We caught a lot of attention from other buyers and the auctioneer who were wondering why we wanted older rabbits, especially the bucks. We did not explain. We hadn't tried our grinder yet and didn't want to look foolish. We kept our plan to ourselves and headed to the hardware store to buy a meat grinder. We had to wait a couple of weeks to make certain that they were healthy. Once the time had passed, we set up the kitchen to grind up the rabbit meat. We had about ten pounds of rabbit to go through. The process went quickly and we were soon frying up rabbit burgers for supper. The kids really liked the burgers and there would be many other recipes to follow. Soon rabbit was on the menu regularly. Before supper one evening, our second son asked if we were having 'bunny burger' for supper! The label stuck and forever more it was never 'rabbit' but always 'bunny burger'.

We wanted to return to the auction for more rabbits, big ones, and fryers. We did not want the kids to refer to the larger rabbits as 'bunny burger' while we were there, so we told them that we wanted to by some of the larger rabbits for the hide, to make them slippers. If word got out that we were making burger out of the tough rabbits, they might become popular and we could lose our bargains.

On our next trip to the auction, we again bought fryers at the going rate, but when it came to the big bucks, the auctioneer had difficulty creating much interest. The price dropped drastically right away. When he got down to $.25 we bought the remaining three bucks. The crowd roared with laughter. We are not sure whether they were laughing at us for buying them or at the price that we paid. Nevertheless, we now had about fifteen pounds of meat for $.75 regardless of what the rest of the buyers thought. And I had enough hides to make slippers once they were tanned. **Lesson Learned!**

Muscovy Ducks Can't Fly

As time past, we decided to buy other types of livestock that were offered at the auction. We ended up with half a dozen chickens, a goat and eventually a Muscovy duck. We bought the Muscovy duck mostly because the price was low. However, we had never had a duck and wanted to try it. Somewhere, in our adventures we had read or heard the Muscovy ducks can't fly. Apparently this was due to their heavy weight.

When we bought chickens and brought them home, we always trimmed their pin feathers so that they could not fly. Since the Muscovy duck we bought was quite large, we felt that there was no need to trim the wings as it could not fly anyway.

Our barn was full now. We had milk from the goat, eggs from the chickens, rabbit fryers, and bunny burgers to feed our family. You cannot live on rabbit alone, so eventually we added chicken and other meats from the grocery store, but our larder was well stocked with what we raised ourselves.

On our return from shopping one afternoon, it appeared that we had a Muscovy duck on the roof of the garage we now used as the barn. Careful study and common sense came into play, deciding how he got there. The only conceivable way was to fly. So much for the myth that Muscovy ducks can't fly! **Lesson Learned!**

Don't Mess With The System!

Inevitably we decided to breed the rabbits, to raise our own fryers. We bought three young does and one young buck from the auction as our breeding stock. Breeding rabbits is so easy that it requires a system to make certain that you know when the does are about to give birth. It is necessary to breed the does at separate times, so they don't all give birth at the same time or you will suddenly have a huge number of fryers to butcher at once.

Our plan was to breed them about a month apart which would provide lots of time for butchering each batch. A system of numbering the cages that the does were in would be all that was needed. Each cage was numbered and it was my responsibility to record the breeding date and the eventual birth of each litter. We also had a schedule for when each doe would be bred in rotation.

As the breeding system evolved, all was going well. The bucks, the does and the fryers were working well together and our system and schedule functioned as planned. I was able to track the progress of each stage and we knew when the fryers were ready to butcher.

As always, there was a "however"!

However, Dad was in charge of the caring for the cages, cleaning and feeding. He was also in charge of the breeding. Unfortunately, one afternoon, he decided to re-order the housing arrangements without a discussion with the 'system keeper', me. When he was done, he came into the house as proud as can be and told me how he had spent the afternoon. I was happy he had fun for the afternoon and asked him to show me what he had accomplished.

127

Once out in the barn, he showed where he moved all the fryers, and the newly arranged does and the buck. I noticed immediately that the number tags were gone. I asked him what happened. He admitted that he had forgotten all about the tags. We now had a situation. Since all the does were the same colour, we had no idea which one he put in which cage. Our breeding schedule was out the window! We would have to wait until the recently bred does gave birth and start all over again. All of my scheduling was useless. I threatened to make him sleep in the barn himself if he ever did that again. **Lesson Learned!**

Enough Of Business

We had been in business now for four years, operating 24-7. It was time for a change. The business was in a good financial position and we should have no trouble selling it. We were tired of all the government regulations and hassles. The bus transportation part of our business was gruelling. You just can't get enough riders to make it pay. Our bus also carried freight which was what paid the bills. The truck we owned also made good revenue under several contracts with other carriers and Canada Post. The taxis were doing well but never stopped. We never had a day off. Even long weekends were busy.

Surprisingly for us, one of our previous neighbours who had always said that we would never make any money, was the first person interested in taking over. He needed a partner to help with the financing. The partner he found, turned out to be the bank manager in town who at one time had refused to help us purchase our Buick because he didn't think we could afford it. When he told us that, we promptly changed banks and bought it with the money we had in one of our accounts. The two of them got together and after some back and forth haggling, they bought us out with great plans for the future of their new venture.

We offered to stick around for a while and train them but they were positive they could handle it. Our previous neighbour was a truck driver and said he knew all he needed to know about trucking. He didn't. The bank manager assured us that his bank training meant he had plenty of experience in how to run a business. We were sceptical. In any case, they wanted to buy our business and we wanted to sell so they would learn on their own. We weren't sure how they would do but wished them well. **Lesson Learned!**

Four Years & One Day

All of my life up to this point, I had been a member of a Military family. As a child, our family moved constantly. My father was posted from the east coast to the west coast and back many times. Sometimes we moved twice during one posting. It was all I knew. We never really had a chance to get to know anyone well. I have no childhood friends like my husband has. He lived most of his life in one area as well as knowing many Military members. I wasn't even aware until I was sixteen, that the men in other families had jobs outside of the Military, like plumbers, electricians, and accountants, among others. I had never lived in one house for as much as four years. If we were going to move again I was not going to leave until I had lived in this house for four years and one day.

When we sold the house, I told the Realtor that the date of possession for the new owner would have to be the date that I had calculated, not before. When the papers arrived the possession date was exactly four years from the date we moved in. I refused to sign the papers and reminded the realtor of what I had told him early on. I insisted that he go back to the purchaser and get the date changed. There was little resistance from the purchaser and the date was changed. We packed up on the appointed day and left the house and locked up on the day AFTER I had spent 'four years and one day' in that house. I had achieved my goal! **Lesson Learned!**

PART 3
HOMESTEADING

It was time to move on. We purchased a few acres of raw land up north, packed our belongings, our children, and the livestock we had and headed north as soon as school was finished at the end of June.

Our transportation consisted of a small, rented U-Haul truck, our van with a trailer hitch and a small trailer. The trailer was configured with sides covered in chicken wire, a few rabbit and chicken cages and a covered top. The goats, chickens, ducks, and rabbits were made comfortable in the trailer. The belongings we were taking with us included a full-sized upright piano, with a full-sized steel harp in it. The piano probably weighed more than the trailer full of livestock. We packed in some furniture, clothing, kitchenware, tools etc. Everything we would need to set up housekeeping when we got where we were going.

We also added a full complement of camping equipment. Where we were going there were no living quarters yet. We would have to deal with that when we got there. Dad was going to drive the U-Haul truck and I would have to drive the van and the trailer. I was terrified. I had never driven a van, let alone a vehicle with a trailer before, but if we were going to do this, I had no choice.

Disinterested Ferry Staff

Since we lived on an island, our adventure began at the ferry terminal. We would likely have to wait a couple of hours since the terminal was always busy. We were directed into separate lanes due to the height of the U-Haul. We explained to the attendant at the gate, that we wanted to be loaded together so that we could take care of the animals. The response was not encouraging. We may even be on opposite sides of the ferry which would be difficult to say the least. The ferry staff did not appear to have any interest in helping us. We were quite disappointed.

Soon after, we were lined up, separated by rows of other vehicles until the ferry arrived. We would have to make do regardless of where they parked us. The loading began as usual, big trucks were loaded first. After a number of large trucks were on the ferry, the traffic was stopped. The ferry staff who was directing the trucks, waved to Dad to board the ferry. I guessed he would be used to space the truck load. After he had Dad moving towards the ferry, he moved the three vehicles that were in front of me, off to the side and waved me forward. They loaded me right behind the U-Haul. They had listened to us after all.

That wasn't the end of it. Once on the ferry, they had us drive right to the front of the loading lane, at the very front of the ferry deck, close to the outer side of the ferry. When we had parked and our engines were off, a worker came to me and explained that I was parked next to a water tap, and that they had attached a hose so that we could water our animals.

When the ferry was in motion, we filled some water dishes for the caged animals and then brought the goats out of the trailer and gave them some water on the deck. The balcony on the upper deck was filled with passengers enjoying the show. In the end, when the ferry docked, as an additional courtesy, they allowed us to be the first vehicles off the ferry. It was an incredible, and unexpected, experience. **Lesson Learned!**

Free-Range Bunnies

A motel was needed by evening. After we arrived at the motel, we fed and watered the animals in the trailer for the night. We went for supper and then to bed. We were all tired from our first day of travel, especially the children and hoped to get an early start in the morning.

The first thing in the morning, we went to check on the livestock. As we walked out the door, we noticed that a small crowd had gathered at the entrance to the motel. It was soon obvious that the attraction was our trailer because there were several young bunnies running around on the top of the wire. Somehow they had managed to slip out of their cage and onto the roof.

The first problem was to find out how they managed to get loose and then fix the cage so they would stay inside. Next we had to gather up the loose bunnies and put them back. It was not as easy as we thought. The roof was small but flimsy so it took several attempts to corral them, catch them and put them securely in their cages. There was lots of encouragement and offers of help from those gathered to watch. We finally had all animals watered and secured but we had lost valuable travelling time. Our trip was planned around having all our livestock securely in the trailer and did not include having to round up a bunch of free-range bunnies. **Lesson Learned!**

Lytton Heat

As we drove north through the Fraser Canyon, the kids enjoyed the seven tunnels that we drove through. I am not certain that the animals in the back liked the changes in daylight as we went through.

Dad, driving the U-Haul was in front of my van and trailer. Suddenly he started to slow down, there was something wrong with the U-Haul. Eventually he pulled into a rest area and got out. The truck was losing speed and we weren't sure what the problem was. We decided to carry on until we reached the next town so he could call the rental company for instructions. When he reached them, they recommended that he do whatever was necessary, if possible, and they would reimburse us after. So, we kept driving until we reached Lytton.

Luckily, Lytton had a service station. The mechanic diagnosed the problem quickly as a broken fuel line. He could fix it, but he didn't have the parts and would have to order them. After explaining that we had a trailer load of livestock, he promised to get the parts and fix it that afternoon. We would just have to wait. We had no choice.

However, this was Lytton, known for having the hottest temperatures in the country in the summertime and this was the hottest day of the year. The temperature in the shade was 103 degrees Fahrenheit at noon and it was going to get hotter! There were no trees so there was no shade. We would have to find a way to keep everyone cool. The service station offered to hook up a hose for us and we could use all the water we needed. Thank goodness.

We spent the next 3 hours spraying water on everything. We soaked the kids clothing and our own as well then we turned the hose on the livestock. They had plenty to drink and in addition to that we literally soaked them with the hose. As the temperature in Lytton rose to 105 degrees, the animals, and the kids, dried off quickly, so we maintained a steady stream of water on the top of the trailer for most of the afternoon.

About four hours later, the U-Haul was ready to go. We turned off the water, paid the repair bill, thanked the owner profusely for his help and drove away from the Lytton heat. We later learned that we had spent four hours in Lytton during the hottest day in the history of the town. **Lesson Learned!**

Driving Concerns

I had been terrified because I had never driven our van, and definitely never driven a vehicle with a trailer in tow. Now that our trip was completed I was very relieved and quite proud of myself. I managed loading on and off the ferry, I had driven up the Trans Canada Highway through the Fraser Canyon and survived the heat wave in Lytton. It may have been a "white knuckle" drive the whole way, but I survived and so did the vehicles. **Lesson Learned!**

Five Ducks & A Dog

When we arrived at our new acreage, our first task, once we had a good night's sleep, was to work on getting all the livestock out of the trailer and settled in temporary housing. Plans to do this were made long before we arrived so we were not anticipating any surprises. It was summer, so our plan was to set up a tent for the kids. Given some simple instructions, they were able to do this themselves while we moved the livestock.

Our property was on a hillside and at the bottom, there was a one-acre pond surrounded in bush. There were five Peking ducks with clipped wings amongst our livestock and the best we could do for them was to turn them loose. We let them out of the trailer and within an hour, they had found their way to the water.

We also had a family dog, who was a collie cross; her name was Penny. She was a good size dog and great with livestock. While we tended to the goats, chickens, and rabbits, she ran back and forth between us and the kids and also did some exploring of her own. She eventually found that the ducks were swimming around in the pond and off she went. The ducks began swimming close to the shoreline of the pond, exploring we supposed. Penny was in the water in minutes, swimming behind the ducks, trying to round up them up and bring them back to us.

The ducks had no intention of leaving the water and just kept on swimming, in single file, around and around the pond. Penny followed, for hours. She finally gave up and came home when it grew dark. We were sure the ducks would return to be fed, however, it turned out that they were feeding themselves somehow and never came back to the yard. Every morning Penny would return to the pond and follow behind the ducks as they swam around the pond until she was too tired to continue. We had no idea that her instincts to bring them back would be so strong and felt badly that we had turned the ducks loose. This routine went on for days, but eventually she gave up and stayed home. **Lesson Learned!**

The Disappearing Ducks

As time progressed, we settled into our new farm. The livestock routine became established, and our children went exploring. There was a lot to do on twenty-seven acres. While resting one afternoon, we noticed that one of the ducks was missing on the pond. We thought maybe it had returned for some feed, but it was not anywhere around. A few days went by, and another duck was gone. We knew that with their wings clipped they couldn't fly away, so where had they gone. They would likely have built a nesting site for the nights, but we had no idea where that nest would be, so looking for them was useless.

We decide to sit out in the evening to see where they would go. Although we sat out for several hours they never left the pond. We went to bed and tried again the next night. The ducks weren't nesting for the night, they swam out to the middle of the pond and basically spent the night there. To our surprise, they were being hunted by coyotes. Our guess was that when they got hungry or too tired to swim they would go closer to the shore and the coyotes would attack and kill them. Inevitably, the coyotes got all the ducks. Turning them loose to swim in the pond seemed like the natural thing to do, but all we had done was feed the coyotes. **Lesson Learned!**

The Hazard Of Gopher Hunting

We came up north to experience homesteading. We wanted to try to live without electricity or running water and to try new things we couldn't do in the city. That meant that everything was worth trying. With our large acreage, there were many things to try, like 'gopher hunting'.

We had lots of gopher holes, so there would be lots of gophers. We hunted many times before and we were both used to rifles. On a sunny afternoon we explained to our kids what we were going to do. They could join us but would have to follow instructions so they wouldn't get hurt or be in the way and they had to promise to be quiet. We picked out a few promising gopher holes and settled in to wait for the gophers to show themselves. The hunting was easy. We harvested seven gophers in one afternoon. Now they had to be cleaned, skinned, and cooked.

Gophers are pretty small with not much meat on them, so it takes a good number of gophers to make a meal for two adults and three kids. We suspected they would be similar to rabbit which we had eaten often. We cooked all seven gophers. They were good. They tasted similar to rabbit or chicken. As a result of our initial success, we went gopher hunting several times. Because our living quarters were not yet ready, we were cooking over a campfire at this point. It was an adventure, but not any different than camping for a few weeks.

One afternoon as we were finishing cooking some gophers for lunch, a neighbour stopped by for a visit. The plate of freshly fried gopher legs was put on the table. Without telling him what was on the plate, we told him to help himself like good neighbours should. It was fortunate that the kids had already eaten and were off playing somewhere. We had cooked seven gophers, so there were eight legs left on the plate, and he ate four. After he was done he said that it was good but realized that it wasn't chicken, so he asked if it was rabbit. No, we explained, it was gopher. He was a little shocked at first, but then he realized how good it was and was surprized but pleased that it tasted so good.

After a few weeks of hunting gophers, we noticed that our hunting was causing a problem. We were hunting on our own property, in a field which was relatively flat, consequently the sound of the gunshots carried quite a distance. All the birds that used to gather around our property singing and twittering all day were gone. No more birds singing in the morning or through the day and evening. The sound of the gunshots had driven the birds away, probably for the rest of the year. We never went gopher hunting again. As easy as it was and as good as the meat was, it wasn't worth losing the enjoyment of listening to all the birds. **Lesson Learned!**

Coyotes Can Be Helpful

As the days past, the rabbits were producing as expected and it was butchering time. We set up an area for butchering. Two trees with a chunk of two-by-four for hanging carcasses and the butchering began. We had a busy day, cutting up rabbit and canning the meat. We had no fridge or freezer, so canning was the easiest way to preserve the meat. When the butchering was done, we built a fire to burn the waste and hides left from the days work. Through out the summer, this was the method we used to prepare our meat supply and clean up.

When we eventually moved onto the bigger animals the butchering process changed. Butchering larger animals took much more time and effort. On one such day, when the butchering was done, we were too tired to get a fire going to clean up the waste products from the days work. We left it on the ground and went to bed. Our plan was to finish in the morning. The next day as we ventured out to prepare the fire, we were surprised to find that the ground was clean. Not a bit of the waste from the previous day's butchering was there, even the hide was gone. Some kind of animal, or animals, had come during the night and eaten every speck of waste.

The next time we did our butchering, usually in the afternoon, we left the waste on the ground until morning and sure enough, it was gone. Now we needed to know whether it was the work of bears or coyotes or just stray dogs. After our next butchering session, we planned a night watch from our trailer, and waited. Around about midnight we had our answer. A pair of coyotes showed up. They ate a good portion of the waste and carried off the rest. They returned a couple of times to clean it all up, but in the morning there was nothing left.

The entire year we were there, the coyotes returned to clean up every time we butchered. We joked that they were being helpful to pay us back for eating our ducks when we first moved in. **Lesson Learned!**

The Taste Of Porcupine

Experiencing new things was what this whole adventure was about. So, like trying gophers, when we were out hunting and ran across an adult porcupine, it was slated to become dinner. Unfortunately for the porcupines, they are terribly slow and therefore easy to kill. However, they are not easy to handle. You have to be extremely careful not to touch the quills. Heavy gloves are required and a lot of caution.

Once we were back home, we had to butcher this prickly fare. Hanging it up required paying a great deal of attention while skinning. Loose flesh with quills can easily get in the way and catch you off guard. Even though it was a warm summer day, we donned heavy jackets and gloves to work in. We did not know whether this was going to be a worth while effort or not since we had no idea how much meat there was on a porcupine. We also didn't know if it was edible.

While doing research on homesteading a few years earlier, we read that porcupines could be easy food if you were ever lost in the woods. The article cautioned that the meat was not very tasty and had a strong flavour of pine from the trees they chewed on.

Well, we were about to find out. First we had to get rid of the pelt. We could not leave it for the coyotes, so we built a fire and burned it thoroughly and buried the waste ashes deep in the ground. We had a piece of meat about the size of a forty-pound roast of beef, so we roasted the meat in one piece. What a surprise! The porcupine roast was lovely and tender and best of all it made a rich gravy that was so deep brown that it was almost black. The meat was the most tender texture you could imagine and tasted like a cross between the best beef and pork you could have.

We were thrilled. If pine-fed porcupines all tasted like this, we should be raising them on farms and eating pinecones. **Lesson Learned!**

The Problem With Porcupines

Hunting the porcupine had been a wonderful experience, but it wasn't over yet. The day after our porcupine dinner, our dog, Penny came home with a nose full of porcupine quills. Where did they come from was the question. We checked the firepit and the area where we had buried the ashes, and nothing was disturbed. We were able to remove the quills, patiently, with some anxious protesting from the dog.

A few days later, she was back with more quills around her mouth and this time we knew why. She brought the porcupine's tail with her. It appeared that while we were busy doing the skinning and butchering, she had managed to steal the tail, and she had taken it off somewhere to bury it. We managed to get the tail away from her and dispose of it like the rest of the hide. We never ran across another porcupine, but with the handling problems associated with butchering and disposal, we probably would have left it alone. **Lesson Learned!**

The Instincts Of Piglets

Our living quarters by this time, consisted of a gutted mobile home with no inner walls, except hanging blankets to divide the sleeping areas and the "bathroom". We had no electricity, no plumbing, and our only heat came from a wood cookstove and a wood burning stove which we bought locally after we arrived.

Our acreage included a large field of hay which had been harvested by local farmers in the past. An arrangement was made with them to harvest the hay while we were there, as long as we were provided with enough bales for our livestock for the winter. In preparation for winter, when the hay arrived, we stored it by stacking it tightly around the base of the mobile home we were living in. It would provide us with extra insulation for the trailer and feed and bedding for the livestock through the winter.

A neighbour approached us one day and asked if we were interested in purchasing a piglet and another adventure began. He offered to pick up the piglet, because he was also going the have one from the same litter. A few days later he arrived with the piglet in his truck. The young piglet was almost like a new pet. The kids loved it. We set up a little hut for it in the farmyard, then went back to our chores. Only the rabbits on our farm were caged, every other animal was allowed to free-range. They never wandered far from their feed source. It wasn't long before the piglet discovered the cozy, warm bales of hay underneath the trailer and settled in. The bales of hay would become the piglet's new home.

The next day, our neighbour showed up. He was concerned, his piglet was gone, and he wanted to know if we had seen it anywhere. We had not; but promised to watch for it. Later that afternoon, we went to check on our little pig in the hay. All you could see in the stack of hay was little wisps of frosty air from his breathing rising out of the hay. However, it appeared that there were two wisps rising up. Upon inspection, we were surprized to find two piglets laying close together under the hay. We had found our neighbour's piglet.

We sent one of the boys to his house to inform him. A few minutes later, they arrived in the truck to take the piglet home. We had no idea how the piglet had found its brother this far from its home. The neighbour thanked us and away they went. At about noon the next day, the neighbour was back. His piglet had run away again. We checked under the hay, and there they were, all cuddled up together again. How did this piglet know where to come and how to get here. They lived at least half a mile away and the two piglets had only been away from their mother for three days. It was very puzzling.

In any case, the neighbour was going away for the weekend, and we all laughed as he asked if his piglet could spend the weekend! Eventually the neighbour was able to lockup the little wandering pig and there were no more visits. We figured that piglets must have some special instincts that led them to each other. **Lesson Learned!**

You Have To Really Want A Moose

When you live in the north, you hunt moose. At least, a lot of people do. We decided that hunting moose was not for us. It is extremely hard work unless you have a lot of help. Usually, they are shot from a long distance and have to be cut up where they land and then carried out. A full-grown male moose can weigh up to 1400 pounds. That means you need a lot of friends or a lot of trips, or both. Either way was too much for us and we didn't have the capacity to deal with that much meat.

Several of our friends hunted for moose that winter, but only one was successful and the only moose we saw all winter was about half a mile away, on the other side of a swamp. We left it there and moved on. One of our friends who did not get a moose said that he had a friend who really wanted a moose and went hunting on his own and he did get a moose. However, the friend did not have a pleasant experience. He had gone hunting alone. He sighted and shot a moose. He gutted it and cut it up. It took him many hours to pack it back to his truck where he ended up spending the night.

As the story went, he had shot a cow moose, which was not in season. The next day he spent many hours as he cut down small trees, cut them into firewood size and covered the moose in the truck with firewood to hide it for the ride home. The authorities up north do not take kindly to shooting cow moose, or any moose, out of season. On his way home with his truck load of "firewood", he was stopped by a forest ranger who had spotted the wood. It is not illegal to bring firewood out of the forest, but it must be windfall or dead wood. There is an endless supply of both in the bush. Unfortunately, the friend was in a hurry, so he had cut down green wood to fill his truck which was just as illegal as shooting the cow moose. The ranger was suspicious of the truck load of green firewood and made the driver unload the firewood, revealing the illegal moose. The driver lost the moose, the firewood, his truck, all his hunting gear, a lot of money and spent a month in jail. **Lesson Learned!**

Winning The Fall Fair

Everywhere you go it seems that they have a Fall Fair. This small community was no different.

To prepare, we needed some entries for the baked goods contest. Dad made exceptionally good peanut butter cookies, so when we got to the fair, he entered his cookies in the baking competition and also a loaf of his homemade bread. I entered a jar of canned peaches. We wandered around the Fair looking at all the interesting displays of local homemade crafts and such that are the usual fare at these events. The kids were entertained by the different events available for them.

A couple of hours past, then it was time for the results of the competitions. There were several categories for crafts and such, and then the categories for the baked goods. There were no names on the entries, only a number so no one would know who the entries were from, just the ticket holder. I was pleased, I held the winning number for second prize in the canned goods. I went up and collected my ribbon and congratulations. I had never won any competition in my life.

The winners for the baking were in three categories: breads, pastries, and cookies. They announced the winner for the breads and Dad had the winning ticket. There was a lot of excitement from the men in the crowd. A man had never won the baking contest before and in fact, they said that no man had ever entered before. When the excitement had settled down they went on to the pastries and then the cookies. Dad also won first prize for his cookies. The atmosphere had changed a bit. Although the men were excited, there were some women there with smoke coming out of their ears. Everyone was gracious, but the women were not happy losing to a man.

The day was not over yet. There was still the Turkey Shoot. After a short break, the Turkey Shoot started. Just to prove he was more than a good baker; Dad took First Place in the Turkey Shoot too. And we took home a twenty-pound turkey! By the time the afternoon was over, the women were discussing changing the bake sale next year to have a category for a men's only baking and limiting the bake sale to one entry per family. We were not popular newcomers. A few sour grapes were left behind. There was a price to be paid for our successful day. **Lesson Learned!**

Campfire Dining

After a few weeks of waiting for our house trailer to arrive, I was becoming very practiced at cooking on a campfire. Breakfast, lunch, and dinner were prepared almost as well as they had been at home. I was able to make the usual campfire breakfast of bacon and eggs, as well as tasty omelets and the usual oatmeal porridge that the kids liked. Lunch became my practice meal. When I wanted to try something new, I made it for lunch and if it was successful, it would become dinner on another day.

When our brother-in-law, decided to come for a visit, we invited him for lunch, and he reluctantly agreed. He knew we were doing all our cooking on a campfire. I don't think he was sure that he should accept, but he was a good sport and agreed. I decided to put together my best efforts and we would try to have a full three course meal with dessert. Appetizers, salad, main course, and dessert. We set the picnic table with a tablecloth and a centrepiece of wildflowers. All was ready. When our guest arrived, we were ready to serve our best campfire lunch. The food was great. Everything was perfectly cooked and there was plenty of food for our guest to have seconds. When the meal was done, we were all pleased. Our brother-in-law was extremely impressed.

He thanked us for lunch and said he would never have believed that he would be served a three-course meal cooked on a campfire and was pleasantly impressed with the quality and quantity of food that we had managed to prepare. He left happy and well fed. We were also happy; we too had never done a three-course meal on a campfire and were pleasantly surprised at how well it turned out. **Lesson Learned!**

A Five Dollar Sheep

There was a Saturday morning auction in a nearby town. We decided to go. We loaded up our children and went to town. We bought a few items that we could use to add to our new home. They were also selling livestock and out of curiosity, we stuck around a while. When they started auctioning some sheep that had been raised by the youngsters in 4H, we noticed that the prices were quite high, well beyond what we were willing to pay. The buyers were paying extra for the sheep because of the efforts of the 4H children who had raised them. Some of the purchased sheep would be used for breeding and would ultimately be worth the higher price.

However, at the end of the sheep auctioning, they offered a full-grown ewe. Apparently the ewe had been well cared for and pampered by a 4H teen but the sheep was seventeen years old. Nobody wanted a seventeen-year-old sheep, so no one was bidding. We bid five dollars, everyone laughed at us, but the auctioneer said "sold!" and we took her home. We weren't worried about the crowd laughing at us, we knew the meat would likely be tough, but we knew how to handle tough meat and therefore we didn't mind the chiding. In any case, it was worth it. We never expected to get a sheep for five dollars! **Lesson Learned!**

Butchering A Pet

Our newly purchased sheep became quite a pet to the kids over the winter. She was very tame, quiet, and gentle. We reminded the kids regularly, that in the spring, she was going to become dinner and not to get too attached. Winter turned to spring and sheep butchering time was fast approaching. Dad and I, when we were alone, discussed what to do about butchering the now 'pet sheep'. Usually, the kids would be nearby when we were butchering and often helped. We figured that they would be somewhat upset to see the sheep butchered. We decided to do the butchering while they were at school.

One day in late spring, after the kids had gone to school, we set about butchering the sheep. We expected the kids to be unhappy about it when they got home from school. They did know that the sheep would be butchered eventually, so we were prepared for trouble when they came home. Much to our surprise none of the kids was upset to see us finishing the sheep when they got home and were actually disappointed that we hadn't waited for them. It seemed that they had settled into the homesteading idea a lot better than we gave them credit for. **Lesson Learned!**

The Last Laugh

The meat on our five-dollar sheep could be a problem. Next came the big test. What would the meat be like?

Usually, older animals are very tough from years of running around and we would have to get creative with preserving the meat. Generally, older meat would be canned or ground into burger. This was the first sheep we had ever had. We had never eaten mutton, either. We had heard many stories about eating mutton and knew a few people who wouldn't eat it because of the palatability stories they had heard.

Since we were up for new challenges, we always cautiously ignored rumors and stories and tried things ourselves. We cooked up a mutton roast for dinner that night and sat down, anticipating the roast to be quite tough. We were surprised and amazed, the meat on our plate was so tender, we were literally able to cut it with our forks and the flavour was excellent. We wondered what all the fuss had been about. We decided that mutton should be part of our regular auction list in the future. We now had roughly seventy-five pounds of premium mutton at the low price of about six and a half cents per pound. We had the last laugh! **Lesson Learned!**

The Nephews & The Rabbit Livers

Whenever we butchered our rabbits, we usually did six at a time. Rabbit was good meat and the kids particularly enjoyed rabbit salad. All of us were fond of rabbit livers, to the point that they were treated as a delicacy in our home. However, if the five of us ate them all at once, there wouldn't be any left for a treat. All rabbit livers were canned for future consumption as a treat or an afternoon snack. Eventually, we would have two or three, quart jars of rabbit livers saved for our snacks over the winter when we did less butchering.

Later in the fall we invited our two nephews to come for a visit. They were about the same age as our boys, and they looked forward to a day in the country with their cousins. They would arrive in the morning and their Dad would pick them up late in the afternoon.

In making the arrangements with my sister, I explained that our kids were excited to share their favourite snack of rabbit livers with the boys. She informed me that her boys would never eat rabbit livers. We discussed alternate snacks for the nephews and warned our kids that it would be unlikely their cousins were willing to eat rabbit livers.

Everyone played hard all day, there was a lot for them to do. We even had a couple of go-carts for the boys to play with. After lunch, our children wanted to have some rabbit livers. No one said anything to their cousins about them not liking rabbit livers. We just put them on a plate, along with some crackers and set it on the table. They all ate the rabbit livers. The plate was emptied, and they wanted more. Since they had just had lunch, we suggested that they go out to play for a while and later before their father came, we would have some more. By the time their Dad arrived later that afternoon, we had gone through two quarts of rabbit livers to the delight of the two nephews who "would never eat rabbit livers". **Lesson Learned!**

The Eyes In The Trees

Living in the country was wonderful. We enjoyed many things, but the one thing we enjoyed the most was the quiet evenings at dusk. We would sit outside in the yard, after the kids were in bed. Seldom were there any sounds other than the odd owl. Occasionally, there would be sounds in the trees. The rustling of an animal making its way through the brush, probably a rabbit or coyote. Dad would pull out his flashlight and shine it around, hoping we would get a glimpse of whatever was there, which didn't happen most of the time. Animals are smarter than that and would hide quickly when the light shone near them.

On one such quiet night, we heard rustling in the trees in the distance. Out came the trusty flashlight and way off to the right, Dad spotted two gleaming lights. He was certain it was a deer. A little while later it was still there. Now he wanted to hunt it. It was deer season but hunting at night is not allowed. He didn't care. Despite my protests, he loaded up his rifle and headed into the trees. He was a good hunter, so he made no noise as he moved through the brush. I lost sight of him except for the odd ray of light from the flashlight.

He was gone quite a while, but I heard no gun shots. Eventually the gleaming lights disappeared. I thought, good, the deer has run off. Soon I could hear him returning from his hunt, undoubtably disappointed at losing his chance to shoot the deer. As he came into view, I noticed that he was carrying something other than just his rifle. When he got closer, I recognized the object and waited patiently for an explanation and the tale of his nighttime hunt.

As soon as he was close enough I could see what he had in his hand was the scythe and he was laughing. He told me that the 'gleaming eyes' in the trees, were not 'deer eyes' but the reflection of light from the flashlight on the scythe blade he had left hanging in the tree earlier in the day! He had been hunting his scythe blade. We joked about having scythe "blade steak" for dinner and then went to bed. **Lesson Learned!**

Goats Love Saskatoons

It was saskatoon season. Our property, as we found out, was loaded with saskatoon bushes. The canning system was set up and ready to go, so we all went berry picking. There were more berries than we could pick, but we set out to get as many as we could handle. The first days were quite busy. We were picking berries all morning and when it got too hot to pick, we returned home and canned all afternoon.

Things took an interesting twist after a few days. The goats followed us out to our location and found the berry bushes. They obviously liked the berries too. At first they were just a little interested and nibbled away at the branches with us. We had to keep pushing them out of the way as we went along. Eventually, the goats discovered that they had a better way to pick saskatoons than we did. They would reach into the bush to the base of a branch, wrap their mouth around the whole branch and just pull back. As they pulled, the berries would roll into their mouths, and they could clean off the whole branch in one move. In no time, they had this method down to a science and were stripping the branches of berries faster than we could pick.

It was fun to watch their antics as they went along and at the end of the day their mouths were purple from all the berry juice. They would eventually have enough and go home but were back with us the next day. The multitude of berry bushes we had was dwindling fast because of the enthusiasm of the goats. We were able to pick all the berries we wanted, but the goats continued long after we were done until all the berries were gone for the season. We hadn't known how much goats loved saskatoons. **Lesson Learned!**

Bribery By Pie

If your sole source of heat and cooking is wood, you need a healthy wood pile. One afternoon, while Dad's friend was visiting, they were planning to go out in the bush to get firewood and take the boys with them. They hooked up the trailer and drove off in my car to an area a few miles away where they knew there were a lot of dead trees. Everyone was gone for several hours.

When they returned, the trailer was full of firewood, indicating a successful wood cutting adventure. However, my car and the trailer were covered in mud and all the boys were dirty too. While listening to the afternoon's adventures, there didn't appear to be any explanation as to why the trailer, the car and the crew were covered in mud. No one would tell me how they got so dirty. Dad tried to appease me by saying that they had to walk through a couple of puddles to get to the wood. I knew there had to be more to the story. Well, he added, maybe they had driven the car through a small puddle too. He was not telling me the truth and I knew it, but no one else was talking either. I questioned the boys, but they had obviously been coached not to talk and had exactly the same story as their Dad. The only one who had not said anything was Dad's friend.

When I finally had the opportunity to talk to the friend alone, I was not getting any more from him either. I decided that this situation required a little more coercion. I knew from past experience that Dad's friend was very fond of saskatoon pie, and I had lots of saskatoons. So, I promised him a saskatoon pie if he would tell me what had really happened. He immediately told me the whole story.

They had driven off onto a dirt road and down the road a bit they came up to a huge, rather deep, puddle to cross. They could have gone around it, but egged on by his sons, Dad took a run at the puddle, which was basically a fully flooded road, and got stuck in the middle. After many back and forth tries and lots of pushing and pulling through the mud, they finally made it to the other side. The kids were really enthusiastic about the exciting time they had and were convinced by their father that it would not be in their best interest to tell their mother, so they were sworn to secrecy.

I now had the whole story. Everyone got a good scolding. Dad asked his friend how I managed to get him to tell me the truth. His friend told him, "You can't expect me to keep your secret when I am offered a saskatoon pie!". **Lesson Learned!**

Then Came The Horse

We had told our children, that when we were settled, we would consider buying them a horse. We knew nothing about horses, but we were in horse country so information wasn't hard to come by. We talked to a lot of people who had horses. We were given a ton of information on what to look for in a gentle horse for our children. It was suggested that we get an older horse which had been ridden by a young person. It would likely be gentle enough for beginners. During our discussions with horse owners, we were told about an upcoming sale of older barrel racers that had been ridden by young teenagers.

We had a neighbor who trained horses and she was willing to help us learn how to handle the horse and give us a few riding lessons. We asked her advice on which one to buy and we were off to the sale. We purchased a little filly named Star (what else!) who had been a barrel racer for many years and we were told she was extremely gentle. We stopped at a tackle shop and bought what we needed including a saddle. Once we were home and settled in, we took our new purchase to our neighbour for our training.

The idea was that she would put the horse through its paces and advise us of any problems we might encounter as novice horse owners. She informed us that our new purchase had a few handling problems and that if we brought her back the next day she would workout the kinks. On our return the following day we were alarmed at how she was handling our horse. She had her on a short rope, trotting her around in a circle. The problem arose when the horse didn't do exactly what she wanted and she would punch the horse hard in the side with her fist to get the desired result. Maybe the horse needed some taming for us as novices, but we did not approve of her methods. We never took Star back to her. Not all trainers are good trainers. **Lesson Learned!**

The Picnic Table

We had built a very solid cedar picnic table years before. It was our pride and joy. We spent hours finishing it, sanding, and coating it in many layers if clear coat. It was extremely heavy, but we brought it with us anyway. We need a hitching post for Star, and it was perfect. Previously, we had no problem saddling our horse, but after the punching from the trainer things changed. When we tried to put the saddle on her, she freaked out. She was afraid she was going to get punched. She was tethered to a solid cedar picnic table, so we tried again. This time she bolted and ran.

When she bolted, she took the picnic table with her down the road. Parts of the table came loose and were hitting her hind legs which made her run harder. The picnic table was torn to pieces. Only the back rail from the seat of the table remained attached to her tether. Eventually, we managed to catch up to her and calm her down. Star had a few minor scrapes on the backs of her legs but nothing serious. The picnic table, on the other hand, was completely unsalvageable. It couldn't even be used for firewood because of coatings on the wood. It went straight to the dump. Never tether a horse to a picnic table if you want to keep the table. **Lesson Learned!**

Beautiful Horse

We weren't giving up yet. We had built a small corral and shelter in our pen to house the horse. She seemed relatively content and had settled down after her adventures with the trainer and the picnic table. Life went on.

One afternoon, while the kids were in school, we sat at the table inside for coffee. While we were chatting about chores, I looked out the window towards the road that bordered our property. There was a horse trotting along by itself. I pointed it out to Dad and commented on what a beautiful horse it was. Seconds later, we realized that the "beautiful horse" was ours and she was loose! It took about an hour to chase her down and bring her back. We realized that we needed to improve her housing arrangements if we didn't want a repeat adventure. We built an improved corral. Horses need better housing than sheep and pigs.

The whole family loved Star. However, after several other unfortunate incidents due to our inexperience and the inadequacy of our small farm, we all agreed to put her up for sale and said a sad goodbye to Star. A horse was not for us. **Lesson Learned!**

Time To Butcher The Pig

It was pig butchering time. Several of our neighbors were setting up to do their pigs and so were we. The usual way to do pigs is to gather several friends to help and then share the fruits of their labours. This entailed building a scaffold to hold the pig, boiling a drum of water, dunking the pig into it, and then pulling it out and scraping the hair off of the hide. It took a lot of manpower to do this and the pig had to be dunked several times before all the hair on the hide was removed. Once the hide was scraped, the butchering could begin. When they were done, the meat cuts were divided amongst the participants, each getting a share. This method required several days of planning and setup.

We were not new to butchering and had a different, easier method. Since we were butchering alone, just the two of us and the kids, we did not have to scrape the hide, we just skinned the pig. We re-enforced the crossbar made of 2x4's between our two trees and hung the pig upside down. We wanted to cure one ham and some bacon, so we cut around the hide down one side and removed the meat for the bacon and the ham. The remainder of the pig was totally skinned. Our method took only a little prep time and the pig was hung and skinned in less than an hour.

The total butchering took us about five hours as opposed to the neighbors' method which took them a total of four days. By noon the next day we were well into smoking the meat and had already set the bacon and ham in brine to cure. One of the neighbours stopped by to see if we needed a hand and was shocked to see our progress. They hadn't even finished butchering and were on their fourth day! This was their **Lesson Learned!**

Curing Ham & Bacon

We were quite proud of ourselves when most of the pork was either smoked, canned, or salted and stored away for the winter. All that was left to do, was to wait for the ham and bacon to be brined and then smoked. It took time for the brining and another few days for the smoking. And then it took a tasting ceremony to ensure the results were good. The bacon was excellent, perfect in fact. We were thrilled.

In a day or two our friend stopped by for a tasting competition of the bacon. We tasted his and he tasted ours. His family agreed that his was too salty, but ours was perfect. However, we were deflated quickly when we cut into the ham. The outer one inch was great, but the rest of the ham was bad. Either we didn't brine it long enough or we didn't smoke it enough. He won the ham competition with a very salty ham, but at least his was edible. We were forced to dispose of the rest of the ham. **Lesson Learned!**

The Pig's Head

Stories travel fast in small country communities. Word got around that the newcomers were capable of butchering pigs. We returned one morning, after a trip to town, to find the top of our kitchen table covered by a really large pigs head! It was a gift, from one of the neighbours, which had been dropped off while we were in town. This pig was twice the size of the one we had butchered. It took us all afternoon just to cut it up and several hours the next day to process it. There were many pounds of edible meat on the head and neck. The kindness was very much appreciated and the meat was thoroughly enjoyed. **Lesson Learned!**

Little Helping Hands

When I refer to "we", I am not just talking about my husband and I, the "we" refers to our young children, aged 9, 8, and 6 years, as well. They were packed up with the rest of our belongings and brought here without being asked. They accepted this adventure without question, and pitched in on everything we did. They took to the farming and helped willingly.

They fed and tended to livestock without question. They adjusted to no electricity or running water without grumbling and they loved helping with the butchering. They would all sit around the kitchen table, knives in hand, and cut meat like they were born to it. We would tell them what to do next and away they went. We had not expected them to participate and enjoy everything we did. We were amazed at how well they adapted to farm life in this new community. To this day, they talk fondly of the things we did and often incorporate them into their own current lives. **Lesson Learned!**

Our Protector

My Mother was among the many visitors we had to our little farm. As I have explained before, most of our animals were free ranging. Whenever a visitor arrived, some of the animals would come and greet them. They were all very friendly and loved to be petted and talked to. My Mother was not familiar with our animals so she was a little cautious but not too nervous. She enjoyed greeting them, particularly the baby goats which were cute beyond compare.

While she was enjoying the animals that showed up to greet her, our dog Penny stood watch. Penny was a pet. She had an affinity for all our livestock but was never trained to guard or protect anything. To this day we are not certain whether Penny was protecting my Mother or the animals. Her protection was obvious when our pig, no longer a piglet, joined the parade of greeters approaching my Mother. Penny placed herself between my Mother and the pig and would not move. I don't think that my Mother was concerned, but Penny was determined. During the remainder of my Mother's visit, wherever my Mother was, Penny was close by to ensure that the pig did not come too close. We had no idea why she was so protective of only the pig, but my Mother was very impressed and so were we. **Lesson Learned!**

Guard Dog, Too!

One afternoon, while we were away, a friendly neighbour stopped by to bring us some fresh baking. Apparently, she parked her car at the end of the driveway and walked up the roadway towards our home. She realized as she got closer, that we were not at home but would leave the baking inside the door, which we never locked.

As the tale was told to us a few days later, when she was about 50 yards away from the livestock pens, Penny stood in the middle of the narrow driveway and would not let her pass. She had been to visit us on several occasions and she knew Penny as a friendly family pet. This day she thought was no different. She greeted Penny as she would have on any other visit. She even tried to coax her to come to her to say hello. No way was Penny going to move. Penny was not aggressive but stubbornly refused to let our friend get past her. She told us of trying to go around her but Penny just moved with her.

Finally, our friend decided she didn't want to upset Penny in case she decided to get aggressive, so she just turned around and left. When she got to her car, she looked back to see where Penny was. Penny was still there, right where she had left her. Our friend decided that there was no way that anyone was going to approach Penny's charges if we were not at home. Our friend told us that she was extremely impressed with Penny's training and what a non-aggressive guard dog we had. We explained to her that we had not trained her to guard anything and we were as impressed as she was. Now we knew that as well as being protective, Penny was also a great guard dog. **Lesson Learned!**

The 'Da Giu' Dog

We had another friend who owned a rather large male Doberman Pinscher. Doberman Pinschers are all 'large' up close, especially when you don't own them. This friend visited us regularly, but not with his dog. He eventually arrived one day driving his pickup truck with the dog in the back. He was enormously proud of his big dog and very aware of the impression he had made bringing him along in the truck.

The Doberman wore a huge, spiked collar supposedly meant to intimidate other dogs, and their owners, we assumed. Everything went well until he clipped a leash on the collar and decided to take the dog out of the truck. Penny had a very strong negative reaction to this turn of events. It was immediately obvious to everyone present, that there was going to be trouble. Our children were alarmed at the sight of the Doberman, and to Penny's reaction. Penny became 'protector Penny' instantly. She barked and growled at the other dog in her territory. Our friend was not alarmed and just kept commanding "da giu" to his dog. We were unfamiliar with the expression and puzzled because there seemed to be no reaction from the Doberman.

When the neighbour realized that the two dogs were not getting along, he tried to get his dog back into the truck but the dog seemed to be ignoring him and his commands. The dog's attention was focused on Penny who was getting increasingly aggressive. Soon the two were obviously at battle stations. We ordered the kids into the house but didn't need to, they were already on their way.

In a few seconds, the Doberman attacked Penny, in spite of the leash and frantic commands from the owner of 'da giu', 'da giu'. We were horrified! Our pet was being attacked and we had never seen her so aggressive. However, much to our surprise, Penny fought back. Make no mistake, this was a truly frightening actual dog fight. We couldn't get near either of the dogs. The neighbour was the only one close to the dogs. He was doing everything he could to break them up. We tried to get close enough to pull Penny away by her collar but the Doberman was in the way.

We told the neighbour to call his dog off. All the neighbour did was keep calling out 'da giu' to the dog, with no effect. Penny was holding her own. The Doberman was scuffling with her but not inflicting any severe damage. The neighbour was actually enjoying the fight! Dad told him to call his dog off and put him back in the truck.

He refused and told us his dog was going to win the fight. Dad informed him that it was unlikely the Doberman would win because Penny was on top of his dog, holding him down and doing her worst. At that time, the neighbour got really aggressive with his dog and pulled him away from the fight, all the while saying repeatedly 'da giu', da giu'. The neighbour left with his dog and never brought him back. Penny survived with a few minor scratches.

We were immensely proud of our quiet family pet and her performance against a large Doberman in her efforts to protect her family. We found out later that 'da giu' (or something like that) meant 'down' in Italian. The neighbour explained that he trained his dog using Italian commands so that anyone who didn't speak Italian would not be able to command him. It was obvious to us that the dog didn't speak Italian either. **Lesson Learned!**

Land Clearing Hazard

We were not the only novice farmers in the area, many of us were from "normal" communities and had taken advantage at large tracts of land that had been listed for sale recently.

We all had lots to learn, many had to learn everything from scratch and some actually should have stayed where they were originally. One such novice lived on one of the larger tracts of land and his living quarters were at the top of a hillside with a long winding driveway. Among many of the instances that convinced the rest of us that he should have stayed in the city, was his land clearing issues.

He wanted to clear the hillside and was planning to do it by hand. That was OK, but he had neither the common sense nor the ability to do it himself. He asked us for suggestions. We had never had to clear that much land, so we weren't very much help. We did suggest that he get some sheep to clear the grasses on the hillside. He would not be doing that. He was convinced that the hillside was too steep and therefore the sheep would fall and roll down the hill. After that remark we stopped trying to help him.

He resorted to scything and it took him several weeks before he finally just gave up on that part of the clearing. He moved on to cutting down the larger shrubs, brush and small trees that dotted the hillside. He created a large pile near the bottom of the hill, close to the edge of his property. He kept adding to this pile until all the shrubs, brush and small trees were cleared. The pile, when he was done, was half the height of the telephone pole at the edge of the main road in front of his property.

Now, the customary practice of getting rid of a pile of cleared brush etc., is to burn it. So, he lit the pile and let it burn. The rest of the community had enough common sense to build the pile of brush in the middle of the cleared area so that it was well away from other things like structures and telephone/power lines. Obviously he did not possess the required amount of common sense.

He built his pile directly under the telephone and power lines that ran from the roadway to his home, about five hundred yards up the hill. His fire was so large that it melted all of the wires from the roadway and half the way up the hill. You might think that it served him right and it did. Unfortunately, when the fire melted all of the wires, the whole community was affected. No one had electrical power or telephone service for almost a week while the authorities worked to replace his wires and return service to everyone in the area. He had learned the hard way what not to do when clearing land and how important a little common sense can be. **Lesson Learned!**

500 Miles Was Not Far Enough

O nce the brush fire at our neighbours was out, the rest of the community waited for everything to be restored. Both hydro and the phone company went house to house checking to see whose power and whose telephone was out. We, of course, had neither to begin with so it didn't affect us, still they came to check. The power company technician tried to talk us into hooking up power but we politely declined. The telephone technician tried the same approach and got the same reply.

We recognized the telephone technician immediately. We knew him, he was the telephone technician from where we had lived previously. Although we were not happy to see him in our new community, we were polite. He also recognized us and was also apprehensive and left after a brief conversation.

When we had run the taxi company in the town we had come from, we were extremely reliant on the telephone system for our livelihood. Our business generated most of its revenue on the weekends, Friday, Saturday, and Sunday nights. Many months before the sale of our business we had serious problems with the telephone company. Every Friday afternoon, at 4 pm, our phones would go dead and stayed that way all weekend. It was very upsetting because we had no revenue at all for the entire weekend. Repeated conversations with the phone company did not get any results and Friday afternoon the phones would shutdown at the same time. This situation continued for several weeks.

Finally, someone from the phone company discovered the problem and the issue was resolved. Apologies were made to us, but of course there was no compensation for the lost revenue. They did explain that the local telephone technician had been inadvertently shutting down the wrong system at the end of the workday on Friday before he went home but turned it back on when he came to work on Monday. We learned later that he had been transferred and we were relieved and went about our business as usual. We travelled all this way to our new home and the last person we expected, or wanted, to see was this particular telephone technician! I guess we should have gone farther, moving 500 miles away was just not far enough. **Lesson Learned!**

Temporary Parking Service

In our attempt to be good neighbours, we agreed to allow a friend of a friend to park his old bus on our property while he moved 'up north'. He would return in a few weeks to move the bus to his new home. When you are trying to be helpful, you don't always check out how these things work. We had no idea how much of a problem this would become.

Weeks turned into months and the owner of the bus never returned. The friend we had tried to help, never heard from this owner again. He did not even know where he had moved to and all he knew was the owner's first name.

We decided to have it towed and would accept that we would have to pay for the towing. The towing company was very understanding, but could not tow the vehicle without the registration, which we did not have. We went to the local wrecking yard and asked them if they wanted it for parts. Same story, they needed the registration. We even put an ad in our local paper advertising it as "free to good home", or for parts. No takers. Next, we had a conversation with the local police department. They suggested several methods of contacting the owner, none of which worked.

Another neighbour, in an attempt to help us said that he knew which area he had moved to and that we could put an ad in that local newspaper. We did that but all we had was the owners first name and the general location. We paid for the ad to run for a month but never heard anything. When we finally sold our property, the old bus was still there, untouched, and overgrown. Now unfortunately, it was someone else's problem. **Lesson Learned!**

Gold!

Everyone gets excited about the prospect of finding gold. There were hundreds of gold rushes at the turn of the century to attest to that. To this day, there are prospectors all over the world still searching for that 'motherload' that will make them rich. Moving to the north, we were aware of the concept, but that was not a part of our plan.

We had a nice gentle slope at the front of our home so we decided to build a barn into the side of the slope. As we set out to dig the foundation for a barn, conversation arose over what kind of soil gold might be found in. We had never considered this before so we did a little research and found out that just about anywhere you would dig in our area, there could be gold. That was exciting and made digging the barn foundation a lot more fun. We were as intrigued at the prospect of finding gold as anyone else would be, but it was more for the fun of it than the reality. However, as we dug, we kept ourselves alert for the possibility, after all we were in gold country.

Several weeks later, we found a strip of gravel and soil that fit one of the descriptions we had read about. We actually owned a gold pan, so we played around with some of the soil and gravel every so often. Then one day we got a little excited. Our gold pan had 'specks' of yellow in it. Now we were excited in spite of ourselves. It wasn't a lot, but we had to know. We drove to town with our little bit of dirt and went to the assay office. I am certain that they had people in there every day just like us. All excited about a little bit of dirt that might bear gold!

The gentleman at the desked asked us why we were there and we were very eager to tell him. So, we spoke up and told him we thought we had a sample of soil that we wanted assayed for the content of gold. We were not prepared for the response we got. The gentleman leaned over the counter and quietly told us not to say that word loudly, it could create a problem. And so, we were quietly informed that in 'gold' country, you didn't go around talking about it, you kept it quietly to yourself because people in general get overly excited.

After our lesson in 'gold' decorum, the gentleman asked us for our sample, weighed it, recorded it, took our name and address, and issued us a receipt and a bill for the assay. We were advised to return in one week for the results and to stay quiet about our find in the meantime. A week later we returned. We did indeed have a small amount of gold. However, the quantity was too small to mine. The assayer told us that the property we were on had good potential but that we would likely spend years digging and never find enough to be viable.

It was a wonderful experience to go through this process. We had a delightful story to tell in the future about how we actually found some gold, but we agreed to quit looking and went back to digging the barn foundation. To this day, we still speak softly and only in private about the gold we found, or any other gold source. **Lesson Learned!**

Walking Livestock On The Frozen Lake

During the winter, the small lake on our property became frozen solid. The ice surface was too rough to skate on but going for walks and playing on it was thrilling and exciting. We had never had such luxury as having a lake of our own. Walking out on the ice one day Dad was followed by his very own entourage. Our livestock were exceptionally friendly and particularly liked to follow us around. Walking on the pond was a new concept for them as well and an adventure they all enjoyed throughout the winter.

The entourage that followed Dad was a remarkable sight. The livestock had their very own 'pecking' order. Behind Dad they followed in single file, largest to smallest. First were the three sheep, next came two goats, then the pig followed by several chickens and bring up the rear was Penny who was keeping everyone in line.

They would walk all around the pond in single file. The goats had trouble getting their footing and would slip sideways and even fall to their knees when their hooves slipped and splayed out beside them. But none of them gave up, they just kept going on in single file until Dad led them back up the hill to home. Who would have thought that these farm animals would be so organized as to who should go first and that they should stay in single file, but they did every single time. **Lesson Learned!**

No Running Water

It was winter and we had no running water. All our water until now had come from a small creek that ran through our property. Now it was winter, and as we had anticipated, the creek was frozen solid. Along with freezing weather comes snow, so we planned to melt snow for our water supply. Snow melting was surprisingly labour intensive and time consuming. We needed to invent a system to melt the snow easier and faster.

Some how we had acquired an 'ice fishing hut' with runners on one side to enable a person to drag it out onto the ice. We gave it a new use as a snow-hauler. The kids loved to fill it and pull it back to the house, resolving a major part of the labour problem.

We fashioned a 50-gallon drum as a water holder with a tap at the bottom and built a fire under it. Filling it with snow was a challenge but the snow melted quickly and we had water. The problem was time and quantity. We spent many hours designing a better system.

We acquired another 50-gallon drum so we now had two drums. We had a friend cut the side out of each one so that they would nest on each other lengthwise, one on top of the other. We put a spigot on the top drum and filled it with snow. We cut open part of the front of the bottom drum to build our fire underneath. We were now able to fill the top barrel with snow easily and constantly. We had a steady supply of hot or cold water depending on the fire.

On our first try, we managed to melt 50 gallons of snow and boil the drum dry before we realized how hot it was. Time to slow the fire down. The system worked great. We were able to give everyone a steady supply of hot water for bath night and plenty of hot water for everything else. Far better than boiling a couple of quarts of water on the kitchen stove all day. **Lesson Learned!**

The Toboggan Slide

If it's winter and there is snow and a hillside, you have to have a place to ride a toboggan. We had the toboggan and a couple of small sleighs and the perfect hillside on our property, just a short walk from home. There were small trees and brush on the hillside that were in the way so we needed to do some grooming.

It took a couple of days to clear a path wide enough for a toboggan run. We built a fire pit at the bottom, off to one side to burn the brush as we cleared and used the fire to warm up occasionally.

Finally, one evening, the run was ready. It was a perfect night. The sky was clear and the stars and moon were bright. The kids took turns, each anxiously waiting for their next turn. Between the toboggan and the couple of sleighs we had, they carried on for a couple of hours before they wore themselves out. Going down was the easy part, but they always had to climb back up for the next run with the toboggan or sleigh in tow. It was getting colder and even with the fire burning at the bottom of the run, they finally got too tired and cold to carry on.

Before they were willing to call it a night, they insisted that their Dad take a turn. Reluctant, at first, Dad finally climbed onto the toboggan and away he went. Of course, he was considerably heavier than the children and when he got close to the bottom of the hill, there was a small hump in the slope. The kids had slid easily over the hump because of their size and weight. However, Dad's weight made the toboggan go faster and it bounced as it went over the bump, and he was thrown a little off course.

Whipping down the last stretch, he was unable to steer and drove right through the campfire at the bottom and came to a stop only a few feet clear of the flames. Both he and the toboggan were fine, but it took a bit of time to put out all the little fires that were now spread across the base of the run. With the fire out, we trudged home to hot chocolate, a good laugh, and a tale to tell. The kids were so excited about Dad's toboggan ride that it took a little time to settle them down for bed. The next time we went on the toboggan run, we built the fire at the top, and farther out of the way! **Lesson Learned!**

Wind Skating

Just a couple of miles away was a large lake which was frozen enough for ice fishing now that winter was in full force. We knew that if the locals were ice fishing on the lake it would be safe for skating. Our little lake was too rough to skate on so we decided to try the bigger lake.

We packed up supplies for the afternoon, dressed in our warmest winter jackets and, of course, brought skates for everyone. Putting skates on three young children was a bit of a chore. They all wanted to be first and all had problems. The boys didn't want their skates too tight. After a short practice on the ice, they were back to get them tightened. Our daughter said that her skates didn't work, they were too slow, but when Dad took her farther out onto the ice and showed her how to move her feet, she was almost skating like a pro.

Our children were not great skaters and the lake ice was a little rough so there were lots of tumbles. Still, they were having a great time. When the wind picked up, they found that they were small enough for the wind to push them along. The boys enjoyed turning around and fighting against the wind. Our daughter discovered that she could skate much better with the wind behind her and enjoyed spreading her arms out so she could go faster.

As the afternoon progressed and the sunshine warmed the air, the kids opened up their jackets and used them as sails making them go farther and faster. Eventually, this became a problem. Our kids were young and their weight provided very little resistance against the wind that pushed them farther and farther down the lake. The boys were the first to realize that the wind was stronger so they turned around to head back up the lake to where they had started. They were struggling to gain distance against the wind.

They soon realized that their sister was still going the other way. They called to her to turn around. She didn't hear them right away and kept going. The boys were panicking. They hollered at her together and finally got her attention. She turned around and tried to skate back to them, but the continual force of the wind was stronger now so she was not making any headway and was actually being pushed backwards on her skates. Now she was frantic and crying.

The hollering from the boys made us aware of the situation. The boys were making their way back slowly, but our daughter was in big trouble. Dad, being the best and fastest skater, went after her immediately, while I waited for the boys. Dad rescued our daughter in short order and brought her safely back to shore where the boys and I were anxiously waiting. There were tears on her rosy cheeks, but she was smiling when she arrived. She was thrilled with the skate back because her Dad put her in front and pushed her the whole way.

Once we were home and warmed up, we asked them if they had fun. The boys did and were thrilled with the wind sailing. Our daughter was not so enthusiastic. When I asked if she had fun, all she said was that she never wanted to skate on the lake in the wind again. **Lesson Learned!**

Santa Clause

Christmas drew near. As with all younger children, our kids were getting excited. Our boys were getting older and starting to question the validity of Santa Clause. The older and more skeptical kids at school were denying Santa existed, as expected. Our kids were young enough that they still really wanted to believe that there was a Santa. As their parents, we weren't willing to spoil those thoughts yet. So, as Christmas Eve arrived, the excitement grew.

Our youngest son always got so excited that he would make himself sick days before Christmas in anticipation. Dad had the Santa suit and traditionally played Santa at several venues and schools through out the community in the past, but so far our children had not figured it out. They even had their Christmas photo taken at the photographers where their Dad posed as Santa for all the young children each year.

In keeping with his tradition of 'playing Santa', arrangements were made with the neighbour who gave us our piglet and only lived a short distance away. He had two small boys and wanted Santa to visit on Christmas Eve, too. They decided to take turns visiting each others' homes, so that the Dads could be with their own children when Santa came. It was a wonderful idea. Santa wasn't going into the houses because the kids knew the respective Dads too well and might recognise them.

They set up the evening so that they would take turns running past the living room window while the children in each household were there with their Dads. The evening started at the neighbour's house. Dad said he had to go check on the livestock and ran the up to the neighbour's barn, put on the Santa suit, ran past the living room window slowly enough to excite the children inside. Then back to the barn, changed the Santa suit, left it there and hurried home.

Once he was home Dad sat in his chair in front of the living room window, with our sceptical youngest son on his knee and the other two near by. In a few minutes, Santa appeared, outside the window running slowly. Our oldest son, exclaimed that Santa was outside running by. Our youngest son, sitting on his father's knee, calmly stated that it was just his Dad dressed up as Santa. In the short seconds that this took place, his expression changed as he slowly turned to realize that he was sitting on his father's knee! It really must be Santa out there!

The boys quickly put their boots on and still in their pajamas, ran out the door to catch Santa. Very soon they were back, disappointed but elated from the chase. They didn't catch Santa and couldn't even find his footprints in the snow. He had just disappeared! This particular Christmas Eve has remained an exciting tale that our children still cherish and have shared with their own young children whenever they questioned whether Santa was real. We learned too, that a little Christmas spirit at the right time can last for many years. **Lesson Learned!**

Time To Leave

S adly, all good things end. Regretfully, at the end of our year of homesteading, our circumstances changed enough that we had to return to the lower mainland and leave the north and our homestead behind.

We spent a few months in rented townhouses and finally bought a house in the country where we had an acre of land and could return to raising livestock again. We actually bought "a little white house" in the country that we had dreamed about on a park bench so many years ago, no white picket fence though, and the stream turned out to be the 'mighty Fraser River.'!

PART 4
THE LITTLE WHITE HOUSE
AT THE END OF THE ROAD

We lived for 24 years on a nice flat, square acre of land on the banks of the Fraser River. There was an old white house built in 1935 and a garage. The acre was framed by a dike to the north and the riverbank to the south. An unpaved roadway ran along the west side, from the top of the dike to the river and separated our house and property from a farmer's grazing cows. There was another piece of heavily wooded property to the east with a small cabin, not visible from our property line.

The dike was lined by a fifteen-foot-deep gully and there were seven large walnut trees running along the side of the property opposite the gully. In the yard, a couple of apple trees, several green gage plum trees, current bushes, lilacs, and a rhubarb plant. The rest of the acre was flat and grassy. It was a perfect place for a hobby farm and a perfect place to raise two sons, aged 9 and 8 and a daughter, 6.

Life is full of things to learn. This adventure was no different. Our neighbours told us that they had always referred to this property as "the little white house at the end of the road".

Fear The River!

When we first bought our property on the Fraser River, our children were all in elementary school and therefore quite young. Our friends and relatives were terrified that the kids would drown in the river. We spent a lot of time, before we moved, explaining the river and where they would be living. We took them there and showed them the rocky riverbank and explained the fast-flowing water and the dangers of falling in. We scared the living daylights out of them. Our second son was particularly terrified and afraid to live there. However, it was better that they were terrified of the river than careless.

As time went by they learned that the river and the riverbank just needed a little respect. In the meantime, they wouldn't go near it and that was fine. Although it was a very long time before our second son would relax and enjoy the river, the other two children slowly adapted to life on the river. We may have gone a bit too far in our effort to prepare them but none ever ended up in the river. **Lesson Learned!**

Tethering An Unsheared Sheep

One Saturday, soon after we had settled into our new home, we enclosed a little lean-to off the back of the garage and set off to the livestock auction. We bought a few chickens, a nanny goat, and a full-grown sheep which we transported in a small pickup truck box converted to a trailer with a canopy on top.

We were able to pen up the chickens in the shed and make a stall for the goat, but what to do with the sheep? There was an old apple tree at the side of the garage, so we tethered the sheep to the trunk of the tree. She had lots of room to graze with plenty of grass. A few days later we went shopping for a couple of hours. When we returned, the sheep was laying on the ground and appeared to be in distress.

She had wandered around the tree a few times and the rope we had tied her to was wound tightly in her wool. She had struggled to get free and now she could no longer move. She had almost strangled herself. The long wool was thoroughly matted around the rope and got twisted tighter in the wool every time she moved. We could not pull the rope free of the wool. We had to hold her still and cut every inch of the rope and the entwine wool away from her body, a little at a time to free her. It appears that you cannot tether an unsheared sheep. **Lesson Learned!**

Black Hands

Seven walnut trees make for a lot of walnuts in the summer. We calculated about two standard pickup truck loads a year. So...we decided to harvest walnuts, to eat and to sell.

We knew nothing about walnuts other than they tasted good. Fresh walnuts have a green husk when they fall from the tree, and we had to remove the husk to get to the walnut shell that holds the edible part of the nut which seemed easy enough.

First we needed to get the walnuts off the ground. A rake and a bucket worked very well. We were able to gather a bucket full in a few minutes. Then we needed a solid surface to lay them on. No problem, there is always a piece of plywood around somewhere on a hobby farm. So, we laid the plywood on the driveway and "attempted" to break the husks and peel them off the walnut. This was a lot harder than we thought.

Now we knew why the crows would fly them over to the sandbars in the river and drop them from great heights! We used hammers and rocks and after several hours, we had one bucket done. We were discouraged to say the least. This was not a viable venture, even for personal use. We started to clean up from our day's adventures in "walnut land". All of us had "BLACK" hands which educated us on where walnut dye comes from. It doesn't wash off – with anything! Try as we could, nothing worked. Not alcohol, gasoline, bleach, detergents, nothing worked. It turns out that it has to wear off. It took over a week to just fade to a dark tan. We would never husk walnuts by hand, again. **Lesson Learned!**

Walnuts In The Attic

We weren't done with the walnuts yet. We needed some place to let them dry out and age a bit. We couldn't leave them outside, all manner of mice, birds and other critters would get them. We settled on putting them on cookie sheets in the attic for a month or two and see what we had then.

We left the walnuts on trays in the attic over the winter. It was quite dry up there, so we figured they would be great by spring. We checked in on them several times through the winter. They looked fine. Around March, we decided to take them out of the attic and taste the crop, such as it was, probably a hundred or so. They were lighter in colour and weight. Good signs of having dried and ripened.

However, on close inspection they all had little, tiny holes in them. We cracked open a few. They were all completely empty! Not a sign of a walnut in any of them. They had been totally eaten. We didn't think a mouse could have gotten in through a hole the size of a small knitting needle, so it must have been some kind of bug.

We noticed after a few years that there were a lot of wasps in our walls and decided that the walnuts had been their winter fair. We realized that on a farm, you can't store walnuts in the attic. **Lesson Learned!**

Goats Like Walnut Husks, But Not Walnuts

The following spring (Easter weekend, actually), we were prepared to build a chicken-wire fence around two-thirds of our acre for livestock. By the end of the long weekend, the fence was in place. We had dug all the post holes and placed the poles the week before. Running the wire was time consuming, but lots of fun. The kids helped (sort of) and our parents came for the day on Sunday to watch the show. By the end of the weekend, the fence and gate were up. We also built a goat and sheep shed, a chicken coop and a rabbit pen. Everyone was comfortable and content.

By the time walnut season arrived, all the animals were settled into their routines. The weather cooled and the walnuts started to fall, and a question came up. What were we going to do with all the walnuts? We didn't have to wait long to find out. The fence we had erected went around most of the acre, including the gully and the walnut trees. All the walnuts fell inside the fence. That was convenient! Well, it turned out that it was very convenient. It appeared that the goats just LOVE walnut husks, but not the shells or the nuts.

By now we had a couple of does and their kids. They would wander around under the walnut trees and literally feast on the walnut husks. They picked up the walnut in the husk with their mouths, chewed a little and then spit out the shell with the walnut intact but without the green husk, which they had eaten. The remaining unshelled walnuts were as clean as a whistle.

There were some harvesting problems with this method. Although we had our fair share of walnuts, after the fact, so did the crows. They were quite fond of husked walnuts. Still, we harvested a good crop of walnuts that fall and even sold some, without getting 'black' hands. Who would have known that goats like walnut husks, but not the walnuts? **Lesson Learned!**

Piglets With Hernias

When spring rolled around, and towards the end of April, we were off to the auction on a Saturday morning. Generally, we would buy whatever we could handle if the price was right. This spring day there were lots of piglets for sale, so we decided to buy a piglet, raise it until the fall and butcher it. We have done this in the past, so we knew what to do.

Sitting at the auction took patience. We didn't want to buy the first piglet up for sale. They were the higher priced stock. We needed to know roughly how many they would be selling and wait for the last few. By the time the Auctioneer got near the end, the piglets were the runts of the litters and many of them had hernias on their bellies, and therefore not a popular choice of the buyers. In fact, often no one wanted them. We bid and purchased two piglets, with hernias, at $5.00 each. We were not certain if we had made a good buy, never having had pigs with hernias and weren't sure what to expect. Because we were buying animals at the auction, we did not know how healthy they were, so we were careful to watch them for a while to see how they developed.

After a few weeks passed, we realized that our piglets' hernias had disappeared, and they still grew and were very suitable for a small hobby farm such as ours. So, now we had added pigs to our pen. The new piglets fit into the farmyard just fine and were a great addition to the entertainment. In the past, it took about five months for a pig to grow to our desired handling size. If they got too big, they got "cranky", especially the boars. Most of our purchases had been boars. Also, we had our own method of butchering pigs and we did it ourselves, so smaller is better.

We were doing very well. Through the summer we had lots of eggs, a family of chicks, two nanny goats, three baby goats, lots of goat's milk, two pigs and many, many rabbits. Most of this was destined for our table - we weren't just doing this for fun! Also, we had made a great discovery for our budget – five-dollar piglets with hernias grow out of them. **Lesson Learned!**

Pigs & Walnuts Don't Mix

Walnut time arrived in late September. Now the goats could feast again on the husks, and we would have a great harvest. Not so fast.....! It was soon obvious that we had a new walnut problem. While the goats were enjoying the walnuts, it appeared that the pigs were too. The pigs showed no interest in the unhusked walnuts as they fell from the trees.

However, our pigs took an instant liking to the husked walnuts left by the goats. Not only did they like them, but pigs are very smart. In no time, you could look out under the walnut trees and see the goats walking along husking the walnuts, spitting them out and moving on. And, there right behind the goats, were the pigs, following along picking up the freshly husked walnut as fast as the goats spit them out.

The goats liked the walnut husks, but they would only graze for a little while and then move on to other things. But there was often more than one goat. Pigs on the other hand, are called "pigs" for a reason – they never quit eating if there is food. That's a bit of a fallacy really, but very close to the truth. The pigs, now about 250 pounds, would carry on as long as they could find husked walnuts. They ate very well and in the end, I suppose you could say we had "walnut fed" pork on the table.

That's good because, that fall, we had very few walnuts to harvest. The solution: we made sure to buy our piglets earlier in the spring and butcher them BEFORE the walnuts started to fall, because pigs and walnuts don't mix. **Lesson Learned!**

Mother Nature's Rototiller

If you leave pigs and chickens on their own to do what they do best, they form an extraordinary team. Pigs love to root in the ground for roots, bugs, and things. They will dig big ruts in the ground wherever they go. That could be a problem, with holes all over the farmyard, but the chickens are part of the team. They travel along behind the pigs and spread and rake the soil looking for bugs and other things left behind by the pigs. Given a couple of months they will plough and rake a whole acre! Mother Nature's rototiller! **Lesson Learned!**

Clearing Blackberry Brambles

When we purchased our property, the gully was very overgrown with blackberry brambles so thick and prickly that you could not walk through them. The gully was fifteen feet deep, ten feet wide and almost two hundred feet long. In addition to the fact that it would be unusable real estate, there was a massive number of brambles.

After the summer heat had passed, we made the decision to clean out the brambles and create more space for our farmyard. We knew we were taking on a monumental task. We rounded up assorted sizes of cutters, several pairs of heavy gloves, and heavy jackets that would withstand the brambles.

We tore out a small section at the bottom of the gully at one end and started to clear. First, we built a small pile of "snippings" and started a fire. Once the fire was going well, we began cutting our way through the brambles spreading out about ten feet in all directions and feeding them into the fire as we went. The clipping was slow-going, and the days were long, with many breaks. When we had cleared a circle of about ten feet around the fire and the brambles were burnt, we built another fire at the farthest end, and continued feeding the fire until the next ten feet were done. It took an exceptionally long time because we had to clear around the fire at the bottom of the gully and all the way up both sides.

As the work on the gully was progressing, we discovered that we had help. Although we had cleared the first section, there were still scraggly remnants of roots, some grasses, weeds, and leafy green bushes that we had decided could wait until spring.

However, we soon learned that "Mother Nature's rototiller" was there to help. Once the goats realized what was happening, they joined us in the gully and started their own method of land clearing, cleaning up the shrubs and weeds we had left behind. It was not long before the pigs and chickens joined the goats. By the time we had cleared the brambles, the goats, pigs, and chickens had stripped the bushes, dug out many roots and raked the soil behind us.

In the spring, we bought grass seed and spread it all around the gully and the size of our farmyard had grown larger. Clearing blackberry brambles was easier than we thought. **Lesson Learned!**

Blackberry Propagation Problems

We did not know anything about blackberries, other than how good they tasted. Having conversations with neighbours and a bit of reading were a good education. Blackberries propagate themselves by growing long runners that bend over as they grow and replant themselves in the ground. Even if you clear the land, they will continue to grow and resprout the following year. You might think that we could have burned them out. Not such a clever idea as we found out. We were warned that burned out blackberries just come back more prolific than ever the next year. The ashes from the burned brambles and roots, just happen to be the best fertilizer there is for blackberries.

So, we had done a fine job of clearing out and seeding the gully, but the blackberry bushes were likely going to grow back in the spring. While trying to find out more about the "habits" of the modern blackberry, we stumbled onto a fact about goats and blackberry bushes. It appears that one of the favorite food sources of goats is, not only blackberry bushes but also, the tender new blackberry shoots.

The following years proved this was quite true. The goats, each year, kept the gully clear of the blackberry shoots, chewing them out as fast as they grew. The goats had solved our blackberry propagation problem. **Lesson Learned!**

Eggs Hatch Into Chicks

You don't need to have a rooster if all you want is eggs. If you want to have hens that raise chicks you need a rooster, for obvious reasons. There is another fact that may not be obvious to everyone. Every egg you buy in the store and every egg that is laid on your farm by a hen is the same as the egg that will hatch into a chick if there is a rooster in the mix.

We had a neighbor who brought her nephews and nieces over to see our farm animals. The kids were fascinated with the baby chicks, so I was explaining that the hens had laid the eggs and sat on the nest until they hatched. My neighbor who ran a large dairy farm and had hens for the eggs, was shocked to learn that the eggs they had for breakfast could have been chicks if she had a rooster. She thought all chicks had to be bought from the feed store. She had no idea that a hen could sit on the eggs and the eggs would hatch into chicks. For her it was a **"Lesson Learned!"**

Only One Rooster Can "Rule The Roost"

Now that we covered the importance of a rooster in chicken propagation, it appears there are a few other reasons for having a rooster and a few things we didn't know ourselves.

As it turned out, just because one rooster is necessary, more, it appears, is not better. We had about six 'banty' hens and one 'banty' rooster. We liked the banties because they were easy to raise and very good layers and banty roosters are very colourful. The hens laid lots of eggs, consistently. To be honest, we had not planned to buy more roosters. But...there we were at the auction and there were two exceptionally large Rhode Island Red roosters for sale and oddly, no one else wanted them.

We could not pass up a deal, so we bought them both and brought them home. For comparison, our banty rooster was about 12" tall, the two roosters we had just purchased were easily 24", maybe more. Also, our banty had been in charge of the hens for a couple of years by now and the brood was his!

We released the two new roosters into the pen and went about our chores. By the end of the day, it was obvious that the two new roosters were not getting along, and we had a real-time cock fight on our hands. They went at each other constantly for several days. One morning, a few days later, one of the new roosters was dead. We felt that nature had run its course and that was the end of it.

Not! Now, the remaining new rooster (twice the size of the banty) decided he was the king, but the banty felt it necessary to protect his territory and his brood. The two of them started at it. We were genuinely concerned about the banty, but we thought that they would establish their territorial rights and settle in. It was not to be. They kept fighting and sadly, it was likely that the banty would lose to the much larger rooster. After a few days of back-and-forth spats, both roosters disappeared.

We thought they had wandered off to recover from their battle scars or had killed each other and were dead somewhere. We couldn't find either of them. Many days went by and no rooster. Then one day, about a week later, we got up in the morning and the banty was back with his hens like nothing ever happened. He looked quite scruffy, and a bit beat up, but he was there, tending to his hens. The larger, new rooster never returned. Eventually, one of our children found the corpse of the other rooster. Obviously, only one rooster can "rule the roost" at a time. **Lesson Learned!**

The Rooster Alarm

After you have spent some time around a farmyard, you will know that there are all kinds of predators lurking around waiting for an opportunity for a meal. Our farmyard was no exception. Predators were ever present. There were mink, skunk, weasels, hawks, eagles and even the odd barnyard cat from the neighbours. We thought we were doing quite well protecting our livestock with our fencing and by paying attention.

In the beginning, we didn't realize that we were only doing half the job. We often set our lawn chairs in the back yard and just watched the show. It was fascinating to watch the actions and interactions of a farmyard on a warm sunny afternoon. And you can learn stuff. One such afternoon, suddenly, all the hens and chicks, scurried into the coop without any apparent reason. They had all gone at the same time, there were no stragglers. What happened?

Then, overhead, we saw a hawk circling the yard. Okay, danger, but how did the hens and chicks all know at the same time? It took some time for us to catch on to how this warning system was working. Eventually, we realized that the rooster is very alert to signs of danger. He even knows when it will rain and whether it will be a hard, long rain or just a shower.

When he spotted the hawk, or any other predator, the rooster made a specific, subtle clicking sound and the hens and chicks, immediately headed for the safety of the coop. If there were any that were out of hearing range, the rooster would find them and bring them back to the coop. He instinctively knew the head count. We thought we were the protectors but in the farmyard it is the rooster that warns of danger. **Lesson Learned!**

Putting Chicks To Bed

Once the chicks were old enough to leave the nest, they ran around with the mother hen to stay safe. When it came around to bedtime, they all crowded around the hen to get back into the nest.

Their nests were three feet off the ground. This is not a problem for the hen, but young chicks can't fly and can't jump that high. We hadn't thought about that. But just the same, some how, there they were all tucked in for the night.

We decided to sit it out one evening and watch to see how the chicks got into the nest. It turned out that each chick, in turn, jumped onto the hen's leg, just above the foot and then the hen fluttered up to the nest. After depositing the chick, she went back down and picked up the next chick. This continued on until all the chicks were safe in the nest for the night. And that's how the hens put the chicks to bed! **Lesson Learned!**

Noisy Baby Chicks

For the most part, pigs and chickens get along fine. One reason the chickens are safe is because pigs have very poor eyesight so as long as the chickens stay away from them they are relatively safe.

However, despite their poor eyesight, they have very good hearing. If you have pigs, there is a genuine problem related to chicks and their 'bedtime' routine. As they gather and await their turn to hitch a ride into the nest, they are very noisy. Squawking, loudly, for attention to be the next one picked up. There are usually six or more chicks squawking in a quiet evening farmyard. You can imagine a nest full of baby birds, only bigger and louder.

This racket drew in the pig. With the sound for guidance, and no hen to protect the chicks on the ground, the pig was able to get close enough to see the chicks and had a feast of baby chicken! He picked them off one by one until they were all gone. Only a couple that had made it into the nest were safe.

In the future we would have to make sure the pigs were it their stalls before the chicks went to bed. It was obvious that pigs liked noisy baby chicks. **Lesson Learned!**

And... Pigs Like Noisy Hens

Even when there were no chicks in the farmyard, the pigs were always aware of the potential for a chicken dinner.

At one point, we had two small pigs. And at that time, some of the chickens frequently flew over the fence into our backyard to graze on the tasty plants and bugs there. We didn't worry about it because they always went back inside for the night.

Our dogs always considered themselves as 'guardians' of the chickens and didn't really bother them much. However, the dog did try to herd them back into the farmyard, but the only way to return to the pen, was over the fence and the dog didn't know that. One afternoon the dog was determined to herd them back into the pen and harassed them more than usual. The hens got excited and started squawking and running into the fence.

The fence was made of chicken wire which has holes in it, large enough for a chicken's head to go through. When the dog chased them towards the fence, they ran at the fence trying to get through, instead of over and they were making a LOT of noise. The pigs heard the racket, zeroed in on it and just ran along the fence line and bit off every head that poked through without missing a step. Five hens lost their heads that day before we realised what was happening. Pigs like noisy baby chicks AND pigs like noisy hens. **Lesson Learned!**

The Rooster Ferry

Living on the Fraser River had its benefits and its problems. We could fish and swim whenever we wanted. Hiking along the dikes and trails was great exercise too. The wildlife and scenery were spectacular.

However, there were problems in the late spring when the river rose. Not every year was a problem, but there were a few years when the water came up higher than normal. Although the river never overflowed its banks onto our property, the ground seepage would raise the water level in our dirt-floor basement and the backyard gully.

When the government built the dike, they used back fill from the properties on the river side. Whoever owned our property at that time would not let them scrape the topsoil from the property, so they dug a gully, about fifteen feet deep, along the back of the property to build the dike. Everywhere else along the river they used the topsoil. The result was that the properties to the east and west of us, were ten feet lower than ours. So, in addition to the ground seepage in the gully and our basement, water would breach from the east property, which was upstream, as the river rose.

Several years would result in the gully filling up but it never overflowed. Now, the problem came because there was a narrow ledge of land on the far side of the gully. When the chickens were on that side of the gully, they weren't watching how high the water was getting. Some years the gully on the east side would breach suddenly from the adjacent property and in a matter of minutes the chickens would be cut off from the farmyard.

The first time it happened we were startled and not certain what to do. There were three hens and the rooster stuck on the ledge on the other side and we didn't have a boat. While we were discussing the problem, we were surprised to see the rooster swimming towards us. First of all, we never knew that roosters could swim. Secondly, there was a chicken on his back! The rooster was literally ferrying a chicken across to our side of the gully. He returned to the far side twice more for the other chickens, until all were safe.

We learned in later years that the hens could also swim by themselves, but the rooster would pitch in and help several times in later years. So, strange as it seems - roosters, and chickens, can swim. **Lesson Learned!**

The Predators In The Trees

We built a chicken coop to keep the chickens safe from predators. The nest boxes were inside and well off the floor and the door was secured at night to keep unwanted visitors out.

It appeared that some of the hens preferred to roost in the walnut trees, about ten feet off the ground. We never had any predators in the coop, so those chickens were safe from racoons, mink, weasels, and such or so we thought.

However, one night there was a loud racket coming from the farmyard. Running outside, we realized that the noise wasn't coming from the yard but was up in the trees. There was a racoon up there after the adventurous chickens. We hadn't worried about the chickens in the trees thinking they were quite safe. We chased away the raccoon, but raccoons will keep coming back until all the food is gone. We lost several chickens before we solved the problem.

We managed to solve two problems with one solution. To keep the chickens away from predators in the trees and to keep them out of the backyard so the pigs wouldn't lop their heads off, we clipped their pin feathers. They are the smaller feathers just under the top feathers. If you do it properly, you can't tell that they are clipped and the chickens can still flutter low and a short distance, but no more flying into trees or over fences! The chickens were now safe from ground predators, climbing predators and hopefully the pigs. **Lesson Learned!**

Eagles, Hawks & Chickens

Amongst the predators in our farmyard were eagles and hawks, "flying" predators, not to be confused with "ground" predators. The riverbank was lined with very tall aspens, some 75 feet in height and our walnut trees against the gully were equally as tall. The farmyard, from the gully to the riverbank, was about 200 feet. The eagles are 'swooping' birds and need open spaces to swoop down and clutch their prey and take off without landing. Luckily for our chickens there wasn't enough room between the tops of the trees for them to fly over and swoop down and then fly out. They did try many times, but none was ever successful.

Hawks, on the other hand, just drop down, grab, and take off. Thanks to the watchful eyes of the rooster, no hawk ever succeeded in getting any of our chickens, but they did try to get the chicks.

However, we soon realized the danger and put the chicks and their mother in a special pen with a wire roof over it. We knew the hawks would try, but one hawk was particularly persistent and stayed a couple of hours sitting on top of the 'chick' pen and drove the hen wild! Our dog finally chased it away. It was good to learn about eagles, hawks, and chickens. **Lesson Learned!**

Blackberry Picking Attire

Although we had eliminated all the blackberry bushes on our property, we still wanted blackberries to pick. In the farmers fields surrounding us were an abundance of wonderful blackberry bushes. All the fields along the road which bordered the west side of our property and our fence line to the east of the property were thick with blackberries every year. The farmers were friendly and had no objections to us trapsing on to their fields to pick all the berries we wanted.

The berries were large, juicy, and easy to reach. Each year we picked many loaded buckets of huge ripe blackberries. We gobbled them by the handful as we picked and ate them fresh for dessert. We baked them into blackberry pies, blackberry tarts, and blackberry muffins. We made blackberry jams and jellies. We strained them into juice and made blackberry sauces and blackberry pancake syrup. We cooked them down to make the best blackberry juice concentrate you could imagine. Just put a little in a glass and add water for a refreshing summer cooler. The uses were as endless as the supply of berries. Whatever we did not use, we packaged up and stored in the freezer for later in the winter. We had blackberry everything all year long.

Picking blackberries was great fun but not without its problems. They are very prickly, and you always want the ones a little farther in, just out of your reach. Going for an afternoon of picking blackberries requires a little bit of planning.

Of course, you need some buckets to pick the berries into and a pair of gloves is very helpful. Blackberries ripen in mid-August, so it is going to be hot, therefore you will need a hat, pants, and long sleeves for protecting your arms. A good pair of shoes or boots are a necessity. If you are avid enough, you will want a small pair of clippers to clear your way to the branches that are just a bit out of your reach.

My mother, being of the older generation, grew up berry picking as a child and was still an avid berry picker. She was excited at the prospect of berry picking so close to our house. She planned her visit every year to come to pick blackberries for herself and to share with her friends who were not so avid or were not able enough to pick berries. We all used ice cream buckets and she would come with four or five buckets to fill.

We would all pitch in for the afternoon to ensure she filled them all before the day was done. We stopped part way through the afternoon for a cool drink and then back to picking to finish off filling her buckets.

My mother lived in the city and was always nicely dressed, even when blackberry picking. I am certain that she got blackberry stains on her nice clothes, more than once.

On one hot August day, after we had done our picking and she had returned home, we received a phone call from her. She was quite calm, as was her nature, as she informed me that she had lost one of her opal earrings while she was picking blackberries, and would we mind taking a look to see if we could find it. Of course, we promised to go and look for it.

The opal earring in question was smaller than the blackberries we had been picking. We did look for it many times while we were in the fields picking but it was hopeless. The area that we had covered that day was equal to a city block and covered in grasses and brush and of course tons of blackberry brambles. We never did find the earring, which was part of a very old set, much treasured by my mother. My mother came back to pick blackberries every year, but she never again wore any jewellery while picking blackberries. **Lesson Learned!**

Green Eggs

Most of our chickens were Comets which are small brown hens. Comets generally lay brown eggs. Like our colourful Banty rooster, some of our hens were also colourful Banty chickens. Banty hens lay pale green eggs! Some people have trouble eating brown eggs and most people do not believe that chickens actually lay green eggs, but Banty hens do. Most of them are a pale green and a few are almost light blue. When you have a hobby farm, like ours, green eggs become quite normal.

Our children grew up thinking green eggs and brown eggs were nothing out of the ordinary. One day, while our daughter (then 10 years old) was in Grade 5, the class discussion turned to the colour of eggs. The teacher was explaining that eggs were either white or brown. Our daughter spoke up and stated she had green eggs at home as well. No one in the class believed that there were green eggs. The discussion became quite animated, and the teacher ended the discussion by telling our daughter that she was wrong because there was no such thing as green eggs.

Our daughter was in tears when she arrived home. At 10 years old she was devastated that the teacher had basically called her a liar in front of her whole class. I was not impressed with the teacher, myself. What a terrible way to correct a ten-year-old. Perhaps he could have handled the situation better. I explained to our daughter that we would just have to give him some green eggs! She thought that was a wonderful idea. We needed to make a statement in the process and teach him a lesson at the same time. So, we gathered up a dozen green eggs. We boiled six of them and left the remaining six eggs raw. In the egg carton, we spread them out, mixing up the hard-boiled eggs and the raw eggs. The teacher and his family would have a challenge trying to figure out which was which. Our daughter cheered up at the idea of playing a prank on her teacher and at the same time showing him and the rest of the class that there were, indeed, green eggs!

The next day, our daughter was really excited taking her "gift" to school for her teacher. I was a little anxious to see how her teacher would handle being corrected by a ten-year-old student. Our daughter returned home as happy as she could be. The teacher had been very surprised by his "gift", although our daughter did not tell him that half of the carton was hard-boiled.

The teacher had apologized to our daughter in front of the whole class, and she came home happy and with a big smile on her face. The teacher never mentioned the green eggs again, but we are certain that he will never tell another class that "there is no such thing as green eggs"! **Lesson Learned!**

Breeding Rabbits

Raising rabbits is easy. A pair of mating rabbits can supply many pounds of meat in a year. Hence the term "breeding like rabbits". One doe can have sixteen bunnies in one litter. Eight is better because obviously there are feeding problems with large litters. In the beginning, we had four does and one buck all in separate rabbit cages. We numbered the does cages as we had done in the past and bred each one. When the litters were about six weeks old we moved them to separate cages and in another three weeks we rebred the does.

By the time, the litters were three months old they were large enough to become dinner. This schedule worked very well and by the time the next litters were three weeks old, the cages were ready for them. This system required careful recording of the breeding dates of each doe based on the cage number. Timing was necessary to keep the flow of bunnies moving along coordinated with the breeding of the does. It was important to record which doe was bred and when. This required good teamwork because Dad did the breeding, and I did the record keeping.

At first this worked out quite well, but once again as time went on things started to go wrong. There seemed to be a problem with the timing, slowly at first, but it soon became apparent to me that things were not quite right in the rabbit cages. After some lengthy discussion with the "rabbit master" it turned out that he had again decided to change the housing arrangements for the rabbits. The does and the buck had been moved to different cages at the 'rabbit master's' discretion and he had not recorded who went where and the does and the buck were all mixed up.

He had done re-shuffling in the past and I thought he had learned his lesson, but he had done it again. He did not know who had been bred because he had not recorded the changes as he went. Now we would have to wait a few months to see which does were bred and then start over.

There were a few heated discussions around the kitchen table over the importance of keeping the rabbits organized and the records accurate for breeding the rabbits. **Lesson Learned?**

Attack Rabbits

Not all rabbits are cute little bunnies. Some rabbits, buck, or doe, have an attitude. In general, rabbits are easy to handle. You pick them up by the scruff of their neck and they are quite docile. Our children often played with the younger bunnies that were as gentle as kittens. Baby rabbits were formerly called kittens. Bunnies get their name from their fluffy tail which looks like a bun, hence "bunnies". Anyway, like kittens that will grow into cats, bunnies will grow into rabbits. Not all cats like people and some cats are quite wild, so are some rabbits.

Sex does not seem to matter. Bucks and does can be wild and aggressive. We learned this the hard way. Over the years we had several aggressive rabbits which we came to refer to as "attack rabbits".

Trying to pick up a rabbit in its cage is usually not a problem until you come across an aggressive one. They are fighters and will struggle when you grab them. They will bite and kick and writhe around. If you hold them forcefully, you may be able to get the better of them so that you can remove them from their cage or do whatever you are planning to do. This comes with lots of awareness and practice, and you need to know ahead of time that the rabbit is going to be aggressive.

Over time you learn that you need heavy gloves and long sleeves to keep from getting scratched or bitten. In the process of learning this, Dad, who was not wearing gloves and long sleeves at the time, tried to move a newly purchased rabbit to a permanent cage. He reached into the cage and lifted out a large buck. As soon as the buck was out of the cage, he raised his hind leg up and swung it down Dad's forearm in retaliation. The resulting gash was eight inches long. The "rabbit master" threw the rabbit back into the cage and slammed the door. There was blood everywhere. The resulting gash was not too deep and did not require stitches, but it could have been much worse.

Unfortunately, working with any livestock has its risks and we all had tetanus shots as a precaution. Attack rabbits are dangerous and always end up as "bunny burger" for dinner. **Lesson Learned!**

Better Homes For Rabbits

The rabbit population was doing simply great. We already had a constant supply of rabbit meat. We started thinking about how we could increase the population with less effort. Always looking for new and better ideas, we designed a plan for raising more rabbits in a domestic "warren".

Rabbits live in warrens in the wild, therefore we thought we should create a warren in our farmyard. We laid out a plan for a pen fifty feet by seventy feet, then cross-fenced the space into three connected pens. The first pen was for the rabbit hutches, the second pen was a feed pen to supply feed and water. The third pen, also with feed and water, was to hold the three-month-old "fryers" when we separated them from the older rabbits and the younger bunnies.

We constructed ten hutches which were installed in the first large pen. The hutches were basically mini lean-tos without bottoms, which just sat on the ground. We spread them out in the large pen, then added some hay for bedding in each one.

The second pen for feed and water, was much smaller and had a small doorway which served as an entrance and exit ordinarily. We created a door which was designed so that it was larger than the doorway opening and would be latched open on the inside of the pen, most of the time. The door, when it was closed, would only swing inwards for the rabbits to access the feed and water. The rabbits could enter the feed pen, but they could not leave with the door in the closed position. The intension was that all the rabbits could come and go for feed when the door was latched open.

When enough of the bunnies were three months old, we would close the door only at night. Rabbits are basically nocturnal, so they would do their feeding mostly at night. The rabbits would come in for feed as usual but since the door was closed from the inside, they could not get out. In the morning, the feed pen would have quite a few rabbits of all sizes waiting to be released. There were no exits in the fryer pen but the fence between the two pens was a foot lower than the feed pen.

We would pick up the fryers that were trapped in the feed pen and drop them into the fryer pen. When all the fryers were removed, the closed door in the feed pen would be opened, and the remaining rabbits would be released back into the warren.

To start the process, we introduced eight does and two bucks. After a few days, we were surprized to see piles of dirt outside of the hutches! The rabbits were all digging under the hutches we had supplied for them to live in. As the days went by, the piles grew higher and spread out more. There were truck loads of dirt outside of all the hutches.

The rabbits we had released into the pen were rabbits that had been bred from generations of domesticated rabbits, raised, and housed, in pens on farms and in backyards, nevertheless they had reverted to the habits of wild rabbits as soon as they were released into the pen. They did not need the hutches we had diligently built to supply better homes for them! They were excavating the burrows and tunnels of their ancestors for homes of their own design. **Lesson Learned!**

Too Many Rabbits

Our warren was working as planned. Production of fryers was keeping up with demand. Our kids loved eating rabbit anything. We had roasted rabbit, baked rabbit, dried rabbit strips, rabbit salad, and rabbit livers, a family favorite. We even canned rabbit and rabbit livers. We developed many different rabbit recipes over the years.

Tanning rabbit hides became a new pastime over the winter. The hides were cut into strips and woven into pillow covers and small blankets. Unfortunately, the young fryer's rabbit skins were very thin and hard to tan and work with because they tore easily. However, we had a lot of fun with them.

As time went on, the rabbit supply kept growing. Young rabbits breed just a well as the older ones. We were not catching all the fryers. Although rabbits are basically nocturnal, some of the rabbits would feed during the day and not at night so we could not trap them. Leaving a few, lingering in the pen did not concern us since we had such a good harvest.

Eventually, we realized that the rabbits were consuming an awful lot of feed. Now, the rabbits were a variety of three or four colours, white, brown, tan and mixed in a wide range of sizes. There was no way to count them by colours and or sizes. Because we had eight does and two bucks living underground, we had no way of knowing how many litters were in progress. When they were in pens, they were controlled and easily counted, now there was no way to count them.

One night, just after sunset, we were sitting in the yard discussing the situation. There was a "shimmer" out in the pen, sort of like the ground was moving. It continued for a few minutes, so we went and got a flashlight and shined it out over the pen. The ground was alive with young rabbits! Dozens of them bounding all over the pen. About eight hundred square feet of furry little bunnies scampering around in the moonlight. What a beautiful sight! And an excessively big problem! The eight does and two bucks had produced more rabbits than expected and some of their offspring were obviously old enough to add to the production. **Lesson Learned!**

Removing The Bucks

Our only solution to the over population was to remove the two bucks first and capture as many of the bunnies as possible. We would have to wait a few months until any new litters were old enough to capture before we could remove any does that may be pregnant or nursing at this time.

It took many months to lower the number of rabbits. Wintertime helped. We reduced the number of rabbits by over one hundred before winter was over, but we still had more as well as a couple of does to remove. We had removed the two bucks to the fryer holding pen to keep them away from the does. They had settled in with their own burrows and were doing well.

Then, the snow came. It is fascinating to watch rabbits playing in the snow, just like small children, jumping and sliding and bouncing all over the yard. Retrieving rabbits was still a daily task but it was more work while contenting with the deep snow. It snowed very heavily one night and then in the morning, it froze and created a crust on top of the snow.

As we looked out the window in the morning to admire the sparkling icy crust, we watched as the two bucks, jumped up on top of the snow in the fryer pen and nonchalantly hopped over the feed pen and into the big pen where the does were. So much for separating the bucks from the does, we should have removed the bucks and put them into the old pens for the winter. Eventually we were able to round up all the rabbits in the warren. We abandoned the warren entirely and went back to cages. **Lesson Learned!**

Ram & Dodge

One Saturday at the auction, a farmer was selling two rams, which we bought. The two rams took all the space in the trailer and were a little rowdy, so we decided to take them straight home and go back to town for feed later.

We had never had a ram before and thought they would be an interesting addition to our farmyard. After all, they are just male sheep, right? The kids were old enough now that naming the livestock wasn't a problem, as long as they weren't pets. We named them Ram and Dodge just for fun. Our young boys were into trucks at that age and decided the rams were built like trucks, hence the names. We were in for an education!

After we unloaded them into the pen, they seemed to settle in quite well and went about visiting the other livestock that they shared the space with. After seeing that they were ok, we left for town to get some feed. While we were gone, our oldest son came home. He wandered out to the pen to see what new additions we had purchased at the auction.

However, because he arrived after we had left, he did not know about the new rams, he was expecting chickens and rabbits or such. As soon as he went into the farmyard, the rams came around from the back of the goat shed and charged at him. These two rams had big, full-grown horns and they were lined up to butt him. We had put an old chest freezer outside of the goat pen to store livestock feed in. Our son managed to jump up on the freezer to save himself from getting hit and that is where he was when we arrived in the driveway half an hour later.

He had tried several times to get out of the farmyard, but each time he jumped down from the freezer the rams spotted him and charged at him, sending him back to the freezer for safety. In our efforts to rescue him, we put some feed out for the rams and while they ate, our son was able to make a run for the gate. Things settled down after that and we were certain the rams had had their fun and would be fine.

We were wrong. They were aptly named. Every time Dad or anyone else went into the pen, the rams lined up for their attack and tried to "ram" the invader who then had to "dodge" both of the rams by sheltering in the goat shed or jumping onto the freezer. The rams were a team; one would come around one end of the goat shed and the other one would come around from the other end and they would try to catch their target between them. They were definitely going to be a huge problem.

When it was time to feed all the livestock, someone had to stand on the stoop at the back door of the house and be a spotter. While Dad went into the pen, the spotter would have to watch the rams and warn him when they decided to line up to hit him. He did get butted a couple of times.

We found out later that the farmer who sold them to us, used to tease them into butting him, then he would jump aside just in time, and they hit his barn wall instead. They came by their antics through lots of practice apparently. Ram and Dodge were not a good fit for our peaceful farmyard, so back they went to the auction. **Lesson Learned!**

Many Pets

When you have an acre of land and three young children, they soon realize that they want their own animals. It was difficult at first to convince them that naming the livestock could be a problem when it came to putting them on the table. At first, our daughter wanted a bunny for her own. That was not too much of an issue because we had lots of bunnies. We let her choose a young bunny and turn it into a pet. The bunny was chosen, named, and allowed to live in the house as long as she took care of the feeding and was responsible for cleaning up after it. We made up a small cage for the bunny to sleep in at night, which was also her responsibility. All three of the kids wanted cats of their own which were provided under the same rules of care as the bunny.

We already had a small dog named Weska, a Pomeranian cross and a big German Shepherd named Duster, by the kids, no one remembers where the name came from. Pet life went on like this for a few years, with changes in small pets as time went by. There were other farms nearby and soon the kids had friends. Our daughter's friend's family had horses. Why is it that all girls want horses? A horse was out of the question. Our farm did not have the space, fencing or barn to keep a horse. There were arguments and tears, but no horse.

Life went on and eventually our friend's father suggested that our daughter could ride with her friend. The horses needed the exercise and he felt that his daughter would ride more often if her friend was with her. He took the time to teach our daughter how to ride and the horse problem was solved. **Lesson Learned!**

Pot-bellied Pigs

Over the years, pet dogs and cats, came and went. One day while at school, a friend asked our daughter if she wanted a small pot-bellied pig. Of course, she did! She came home begging and pleading that she would take care of the pig. After all we had lots of pigs over the years, why not a pet pig. After much discussion, we said she could have the pig, but the pet rules would apply to the pig, it was her responsibility. Yes! Yes! Yes! Of course. Our daughter was incredibly good at caring for her pets in the past so we were confident she could handle the pig, too.

Our pigs were generally easy to handle so we did not anticipate any problems with this pig. The pig lived in the farmyard most of the time, especially during the day while our daughter was in school. After school she would take him for walks. She had a large dog collar and a leash. The pig was about the size of a large bulldog, so the collar was a good fit. He came from a family who had acquired him for a pet as a piglet but now he was too big to be a house pet like most cute, little pot-bellied pigs, they get bigger.

However, he was much more friendly than our auction pigs. After a while he got bored with the farmyard and after going for walks with our daughter all the time, he decided to go exploring on his own. Our fence was relatively well built to keep the animals in, but we did not plan on them going under the fence. Only the posts were in the ground, not the wire. Like any other pig, this one could plow up the ground with little effort, he just decided to do it under the fence. And he was off!

Dad realized at some point in the afternoon that the pig was missing and eventually found the hole he had excavated under the fence. So, we stopped what we were doing, grabbed the leash and some feed in a bucket and went for a walk. The easiest way to round up a pig is to put some food in front of him. We scoured the neighbourhood, talked to the neighbours, and finally tracked him down. He was not ready to go home yet and took off as soon as he saw us. We searched for a long time before we gave up and went home.

When the kids came home from school, we sent them out to find the missing pig. About an hour later they were back with the pig which our son had managed to corner and catch. As the days went on this became a regular after-school activity. Every few days the pig would dig himself out of the pen and take off. Our children were well practiced now at looking, finding, and catching the pig, but he was smarter, too and it took much longer to capture him.

He could often be found next door, sleeping in the hay under one of the horses. Finally, the boys had enough and refused to chase him any longer. Our daughter was frustrated as well. Coming back with the pig, totally exhausted, one afternoon, she handed the pig on the leash to her Dad and said, "Dad, just shoot him". End of the pet pot-bellied pigs. **Lesson Learned!**

Peacocks & Pheasants

One summer, Dad worked on a school construction site. A peacock wandered onto the site and became a nuisance. Catching the peacock turned into a time-consuming problem. The crew tried rounding up the peacock every day for weeks. Eventually they were successful and then did not know what to do with the peacock, so it ended up in our farmyard.

The peacock was incredibly beautiful and showy but was very wild. He was also quite aggressive to the other livestock and often attacked any animal that came near. Eventually, he just died. We do not know why, but one morning he was laying on the ground dead.

Later in that same summer we bought a pheasant at the auction. He too, was very colourful and very wild. We did not trim his wings before we turned him loose in the yard, consequently he eventually flew over the fence and out into the surrounding community and we never saw him again. Peacocks and pheasants were not a good fit for our farmyard either. **Lesson Learned!**

What Ducks Do Best

At the auction, we bought a full grown, domestic white, Pekin duck. Although the duck was destined for dinner eventually, he was a welcome addition to the farmyard. He fit in well with the rest of the livestock and our children, especially our daughter, enjoyed playing with him and was able to pick him up and carry him around.

One afternoon, the thought came to our kids that he would love to swim in our backyard swimming pool. Not the best idea, but they put him in the pool anyway. The duck was in his element. He swam and dove for hours, and the kids were as thrilled as the duck. Later in the afternoon, he had to come out of the pool. Since our daughter was his "best friend", she put on her bathing suit and was in charge of getting him out of the pool. It took a while; he did not want to leave. It had been an entertaining afternoon but now we had to clean the pool to get rid of the droppings, dirt, and feathers. A few days went past, and all was well until mid-afternoon about a week later. The duck was back in the pool. We had not trimmed his feathers and he had flown over the fence and into the pool. He enjoyed his afternoon swim and when he was finally captured and removed from his swim, his feathers were trimmed to prevent future trips to what had quickly become his 'duck pond'. He was just doing what ducks do best. **Lesson Learned!**

The Eagle Hunt

L iving on the river, meant we could go fishing whenever we wanted, and we spent many hours on the riverbank. It was a wonderful way to spend the afternoon. Sometimes we caught fish and sometimes we did not. It did not matter. We were not avid fishermen. Just a rod, a reel, and a few worms. Sitting on the bank, we would watch the river world go by. There were the occasional river otters, lots of fish jumping, as well as birds flying overhead constantly.

On a mid-summer afternoon, while we were fishing, we noticed a young gosling on the river, just upstream. It was alone, no other geese were on the water around it. Somehow it had become separated from the rest of the brood. All of a sudden, as it floated along, trying to stay afloat in the river current, an eagle dived out of the sky from upstream and attacked it and then took off. A few seconds later, another eagle came from downstream, and it also attacked the gosling, then flew away upstream. The eagles repeated this pattern over and over. It became apparent that the two eagles were taking turns harassing the poor little gosling.

There was not a thing we could do to help the young bird; it was too far from shore and the river was too deep and moving fast. The eagles continued their plan of attack, taking turns from upstream and downstream, each one attacking the gosling in turn. It was hard to watch as Mother Nature took her course. Finally, the gosling stopped fighting. The eagles made a couple of more attacks, then one of them dived into the water, captured the gosling and flew away. We did not know that eagles would attack in pairs and hunt like that in water. **Lesson Learned!**

Let's Go Fishing

Once our children all had fishing rods, they would sit on the rocks and try to catch fish. Most of the time they caught bottom fish or just got snagged. They were quite young and not patient fisherpersons. They became frustrated easily and wanted to go somewhere else to fish.

On a nice fall Sunday morning, we packed up our fishing gear, a picnic lunch and the kids and drove off to find a nice quiet lake for the kids to fish in. Before the day was over we had been to five different fishing places. The kids were not happy, they did not catch any fish.

Since the day wasn't over yet, when we got home they wanted to spend some time on the riverbank. It was perfect timing; the fish were biting, and they all caught fish before supper. After supper they were right back at it. Between the three of them they had caught a couple more fish before dark.

Before they went to bed that night, they realized that we had spent an entire day driving all over the valley and the best fishing was in their own backyard. **Lesson Learned!**

The Salmon Run

Fraser River salmon runs are the largest in the world. Millions of salmon swim upriver to spawn each year. People gather along the banks to watch the salmon migration.

Living on the Fraser River gave us a unique advantage. We could sit on the bank of the river with a picnic lunch, kids, and pets, in awe of the sheer numbers of salmon roiling up the waters as they fought the current. The spring run-off will subside in the fall and the water will be low enough to allow sandbars to rise just off the riverbank.

Walking along the sandbars in the fall and winter was always a wonderful way to spend the afternoon. If nature allows, the water will be low enough for small sandbars to poke up through the water current during a salmon run. Salmon swimming up stream will wriggle, flop, and jump to try to make their way along the edges of the sandbars in their path, putting on a great show for anyone lucky enough to be there to see them.

Living on the banks of the Fraser River during the biggest salmon run in the history of the Fraser River was unbelievable! The entire run lasted for several months. During the best of the run, hundreds of thousands of salmon swam past our vantage point every hour. One afternoon, when the water was at its lowest, a sandbar appeared about twenty-five feet from the riverbank. It was at least thirty feet wide and as long as a city block. We gathered our fishing gear and rubber boots and headed out. Smaller sandbars often appear along the shoreline and create bridges to the larger sandbars. If you pay attention to the tide, you can often spend three or four hours on the big sandbars while the tide is out.

The salmon were there in immense numbers, swimming along the outer edge of the sandbar as far as you could see. We walked into the water at the edge of the sand and cast our lines. We didn't expect to catch any salmon, we only had regular fishing line and lures, nothing intended for avid salmon fishing. We lost a lot of line and all of our lures. Eventually, we quit trying.

Stunned and awed by the shear numbers of salmon, we were standing about four or five feet out from the edge of the sandbar, in almost two feet of water. We looked down at our feet and there were salmon literally swimming all around us, in front and in back. All you could see was a solid wall of salmon. We were standing in the middle of thousands of spawning salmon. It was breathtaking!

The tide was coming in and we knew it was time to leave, and as we turned to go, a salmon jumped out of the water and onto the sand, beaching itself, then another and another. We spent a few minutes trying to get them back into the water. There were too many and the water was rising so we had to leave them and hope that nature would get them back into the river as the tide came in. The whole afternoon, walking amongst the once-in-a-lifetime salmon run was amazing. **Lesson Learned!**

Buckets Of Ooligans

The salmon run is not the only fish run on the Fraser River. In the late spring, there is an ooligan run. Ooligans are like smelts and they used to run in numbers that rivaled the salmon run. Unfortunately for us, we did not know this when first we moved there. We eventually heard of the ooligans and the ooligan run from our neighbours. The neighbours did not fish for ooligans, so it took a little researching to find out what ooligan fishing was all about.

Apparently, they were a staple of local native tribes, especially in the spring when winter supplies were low. So, now where were they, how do you fish for them and how do you eat them. It was hard to find answers. We eventually found out that all you need is a bucket to dip in the water and you can pull them up by the bucket full. Really?

Most years that we lived on the Fraser River we did not see or hear anything about the ooligan run. Most of the ooligan runs were out in the channel and we did not have a boat. One year however, the ooligan run was coming upriver along the riverbank and was going to go right past our farm. The children were thrilled. Fish by the bucket full is what the neighbour told them.

We had to round up three ice cream buckets and tie rope handles on them. We also needed a tub to dump the buckets into. We were afraid that the children were going to be disappointed. We had never heard of fish by the bucket full. It seemed a bit unrealistic and thought maybe the neighbour was pulling their legs.

The ooligan run began. At first there were only a few and there were frowns all around. A couple of days later, in the late afternoon, the kids were squealing with delight! Their buckets were, indeed, full. Again, and again the buckets came up full of ooligans! In no time at all the tub was full. They had to stop fishing. We had more ooligans than we could handle.

It took us many months to eat up or give away all the ooligans they had caught in one short afternoon. We were never able to fish for ooligans again. These plentiful little fish never returned so close to our riverbank, but the kids had the time of their lives that afternoon. **Lesson Learned!**

Sandbar Campers

In the area of the Fraser River where we lived, there is a three-foot tide that rises and falls every eight hours, the same as the ocean. Sandbars start to appear as the tide goes out and usually disappear again during high tide. Most first-time river visitors do not know this. Where we sat on the riverbank edging our property, we could see across the river to a large sandy section of beach on the other side. We spent many evenings in late summer, sitting on the bank while fishing, watching, and listening to the campers and fishermen on the other side. We could not hear what they were saying but they were often quite rowdy. They also played loud music and sang a lot.

Occasionally, there would be small sandbars just off the shore at low tide and adventurous campers would load their gear in a small boat or a canoe in the late afternoon and paddle out to the sandbar. They would set up their camp for the night, unaware of the danger they were in. Invariably, the tide would creep up the sandbar. While they were sitting around a campfire enjoying the evening, they did not notice the tide coming in. Usually, their first clue was when the boat they came in, started floating away. Everything suddenly became loud and anxious. Friends and strangers on the shore would shout out to them trying to tell them that their boat was floating away. Once the campers realized the danger they were now in, there was a panicked scramble to pack their things and to get off what was left of the sandbar! With help from those on the shore, most of the campers got back to solid ground on their own. Once, someone called the police for assistance, but we never heard of anyone who drowned.

However, in all the years we lived there, most of the sandbar campers lost a lot of their gear and a few had to recover their boats down stream. We doubt that they ever camped on the Fraser River sandbars again. **Lesson Learned!**

Sandbar Fishermen

ishermen line the Fraser River all year round, especially in the late summer and early fall. Many of them who fish there often, are aware of the tides. They will fish from the sandbars knowing that time is limited, and they have to leave before high tide. Over the years, we only had one incident near by when the fisherman was caught off guard because he was unaware of the tide.

A young man and his two young sons made their way out to a large sandbar by way of smaller sandbars along the shore. They were loaded with gear, lawn chairs and a cooler. They picked a nice spot on the outer edge of the sandbar and settled in for an afternoon of river fishing. Sandbars are great fun for young children who have a very short attention span for fishing. Dad was able to fish and did not have to worry that the boys would wander off.

We watched them arrive, and assuming that Dad was aware of the tide, we went back to whatever we were doing that afternoon. A few hours later, our oldest son came to us, concerned about the man and the boys on the sandbar. The tide was coming in and the sandbars along the shore were starting to disappear. The Dad was obviously unaware of the diminishing size of the sandbar they were on and did not show any signs of planning to leave, and they would soon be stranded when their exit route was under water.

We sent our boys down to the riverbank nearest the sandbar to "remind" the Dad that the tide was coming in and he would soon be stranded. The Dad was irritated that these young boys would harass him. He yelled at them to go away and leave them alone. Our boys left but we watched the water rising until it was obvious that they were really in trouble. The river had risen enough and the only way off the sandbar was through the river current.

My husband and the boys took some rope and went back to where the Dad and boys had crossed the river. After a short, terse discussion with the Dad, he realized what had happened and how much trouble he and his boys were in. The boys were terrified and crying. They gathered up their gear, chairs, and cooler, walked off what was left of the sandbar and waded into the water.

The water, by now, was up to the boys' waists and moving fast. They soon lost the cooler, some fishing gear and one chair. My husband threw the rope to the Dad, who had the boys hang on to it as they made their way to shore. When everyone was safe, the Dad thanked my husband and the boys for saving them. He told them that he did not know about the tide and apologised to them for not listening. **Lesson Learned!**

Helicopter Pilot Training

For a couple of years, the Fraser River did not have high water in the spring, so in late summer and early fall the sandbars sprung up and grew in size. We witnessed lots of activity on the sandbars but none as entertaining as the training of helicopter pilots. One of the local flying schools took advantage of the long, solid sandbars for training novice pilots how to land.

The Fraser River in this area was wider than anywhere in the lower mainland and relatively unpopulated. The sandbars were long, wide and near the middle of the river. Our weekend afternoons were spent sitting on the bank watching the new pilots practicing their landings. They would approach the end of the sandbar and try to land smoothly. The newer the pilot the more they bounced. Most would not succeed on the first try and would have to go back up and swing around for another try. They would practice three or four times until their instructor was satisfied and then the helicopter would leave. Sometimes you could feel the frustration of the pilot and instructor as they tried repeatedly, but they eventually succeeded.

We thought that the instructors and pilots must have had a relatively good relationship and patience with each other to withstand all the practice landings that some of the new pilots had to go through. There was an exception though. One afternoon the landings were particularly rough and frequent. We thought that perhaps this pilot was never going to get his landings right. Finally, they set the helicopter down on the sand, turned the motor off and both doors opened. The pilot came out one door and the instructor came out the other door and they walked away in opposite directions. We suspected that things were not going too well in the cockpit!

After about fifteen minutes, they both returned to the helicopter and got into their respective seats. They sat there quietly for about another fifteen minutes. The motor started up and the helicopter lifted off. They made a circle above the sandbar and took another attempt at a landing. It was a perfect landing this time. The pilot repeated the perfect landing twice more and then the helicopter left. It looked to us like the pilot's difficult day had ended successfully. **Lesson Learned!**

Planes On The River

Helicopters were not the only aircraft using the sandbars when the river was this low and the tide was out. These sandbars were large enough to land a small private airplane.

At one point, we were treated to two private planes that would arrive late in the afternoon on a Tuesday. One plane would land and several minutes later a second plane would land. The pilots would leave their planes and have a few minutes of conversation before returning to their planes and then taking off in turn and leaving.

At first, we enjoyed watching these events. However, after a few weeks it soon became clear that they were landing on the sandbar on the same day and time every week. All they did was land, chat and take off. We thought the routine was suspicious. We notified the local police department, and they showed up at our home the following Tuesday to observe the odd behavior.

The police, although interested, asked a few questions but said very little to us when they left. We decided they probably weren't concerned. To our surprise, the next Tuesday, after the visitors arrived and landed on the sandbar, so did a police helicopter and three police boats. Guns were drawn and there was some yelling and a bit of a scuffle, but the police had the pilots in custody, loaded them into the helicopter and left.

Someone piloted the planes as they left, but not the pilots that landed them! We were informed a few days later that they were dealing in drugs. Not all of the adventures on our little stretch of the Fraser River were good ones. **Lesson Learned!**

Canada Geese Molting Season

Living on a small hobby farm on the river was wonderful. Our farm was isolated from the neighbours and local traffic. Other than wildlife and an occasional herd of cows across the road it was peaceful and quiet, especially at night. For the first few years this was the way it was all year round. As it turned out, it was not always going to be "quiet".

We soon realized that there are exceptions to all things in nature. During our first years, the water level in the Fraser River was high enough that there were seldom sandbars of consequential size. Occasionally there were small sandbars along the banks that came a went with the tides during the fall and winter. Some years the water level in the Fraser River was unusually low and large sandbars appeared just out from the riverbank that lined our property.

One summer night just after going to bed, we began to hear geese honking and wondered what all the fuss was about. The noise got louder and louder until we had to get up and investigate. Our kids were up too. We all ventured out to the riverbank where the noise was coming from. What a surprise! There were a least a hundred Canada Geese collecting on the sandbar about fifty feet out in the river. They were all moving around, flapping their wings, and honking constantly and there were more landing every minute. The geese stayed all night and never stopped honking and squawking. It was hard to sleep.

The geese left at dawn, and we were grateful for the quiet, and happy that they had left. Thank goodness they were gone. We were not as fortunate as we thought. The geese returned almost every night for six weeks. There were some nights when the tides interfered with the size of the sandbar, but they were short lived.

It turns out that Canada Geese molt for six weeks every summer and they gather in large flocks for protection at night. The sandbar was an immense size and perfect for protection during their molt. Some years were not going to be as quiet as we expected. **Lesson Learned!**

The September Sandbar

The riverbank in front of our property was lined with large rock put there to protect the bank from erosion by the river. Farther up-river, the bank is less protected, allowing easy access to the small sandbars that sometimes line the edge. These small sandbars were great fun for our children once they learned the dangers of the tides. They would play for hours and often.

On a sunny late September Sunday afternoon all three went down to the sandbars to play. A couple of hours later they came home cold, tired, wet, and covered in river sand and muck as usual. All three needed showers and clean, dry clothes. The next day they left for school. When they returned from school, our daughter was not well. At first we thought she had a cold, but soon it was obvious there was a more severe problem because she was having trouble breathing.

After talking to her brothers about the previous afternoon's adventures on the sandbar, we knew she had a problem. The afternoon before on the sandbar they had buried her completely, up to her neck, in the cold, wet river sand. A visit to the Doctor's office and a few tests confirmed our suspicions, she had pneumonia. Never again did they bury anyone of them in a September sandbar. **Lesson Learned!**

The Creek

L iving on the Fraser River had its benefits but living on any river has its drawbacks. High water is the main threat. The Fraser River floods its banks every few years. Most often it is mild flooding in lowlands but there are years when the river is a major threat to the inhabitants all along the river. We were aware of the threat to our property even though we were on relatively high ground. There was "high" water each year during the spring run-off from the mountains. In all the years we lived on the river, the water never rose high enough to wet the grass on our lawn. The river did come very close a couple of times.

One problem we did have, was that only half of our basement walls were encased in concrete and the floor and remainder of the basement was dirt with only a partial foundation. We had a pump to empty out the river water that was often high enough to allow water to get into the basement through seepage. River water seeped into the fifteen-foot-deep gully, which ran along the north side of our property, just about every year, because the bottom of it was so much lower than the basement. The fun part of the gully seepage was that it created a small swimming pool for the kids for a few short weeks. The gully would empty slowly as the river water subsided and everything would go back to normal.

We hadn't lived there for too many years when the first high water threatened the valley. We were used to the gully seepage levels by then, so we thought there were no surprises coming. Since the property to the east of us was a few feet lower than our property, the river occasionally poured on to it when the water rose unusually high. We were still dry, but the seepage in the gully was a bit more than other years. We felt that with the rate of the seepage, the gully would likely maintain its current level for some time.

Then one afternoon our daughter rushed into the house and proclaimed to her father that "the creek is running". He responded, "We don't have a creek". Her response: "We do now!". Sure enough, when we all hurried out to the east end of the gully, water was rushing in from a small dip in the end of the gully leading to the property next door. It took less than a day for the 'creek' to fill the 200-foot-long gully with almost fifteen feet of river water creating a huge swimming pool. Never assume that you know what a rising river will do. **Lesson Learned!**

The High Water Mark

Every year we recorded the high-water levels at our property on a tree on the riverbank. We had our own 'high-water' mark which was usually a little lower or higher than the government's gauge down stream. Marking the high-water became a ritual each year. Eventually a year came when the river rose so much that we couldn't reach the tree with the marks on it. There was just too much water between the land and the tree. We did mark the water level on a closer tree, but it wasn't quite the same. Then they warned us that the river was going to rise even more, and the new tree would be unreachable. When the river reached its peak that year, the water was so high that our daughter stood at the end of the road in front of our house with her toes touching the water and we took a picture of our new "high-water" mark. **Lesson Learned!**

High Water Trains

On the other side of the river from our little farm was a four-lane highway and a set of railway tracks. The noise from the trains and highway traffic were very muted due to the distance from us and the height of the riverbank. In the winter when the air was crisp and clear, and if we listened carefully, we could hear sirens on the freeway and the occasional train going by. Most of the time we were unaware of the activity across the river. Even in years when the river rose in the spring, the sounds from across the river were muted.

The situation changed one year when the river was exceptionally high. When we went to bed at night and the air was still, you could hear vehicle traffic on the highway and most of the trains going by. As the river rose even more the sounds became louder, but not enough to keep us awake at night. Because we could sleep through the sounds, we thought very little about the noise.

Until one night at the height of the river's high-water level, we were awakened by the sound of a train. It was the loudest train we had ever heard, and it sounded like it was coming through our bedroom window! The height of the river full of water and the still air was amplifying the sound of the trains from across the river. It was deafening and startled everyone out of their sleep. It was truly terrifying in the first seconds before we realized what was happening. The trains came "through the bedroom window" a few more times that year. We had no idea that the high-water could cause that much amplification. **Lesson Learned!**

The Bradshaw Plum Tree

With an acre of land to work with, we had to have a garden. I was not a great gardener, but I did try. We prepared a small plot for vegetables and had some successes each year. I also planted flowers all around the house over the years. The place looked nice and cheery but not as good as I would have liked.

My mother was a great gardener and each year she would bring me plants that she no longer wanted in her garden, and I would plant them in mine. They did surprisingly well compared to my usual fare. She often complemented me on how much better they grew in my garden. I always thought she was exaggerating to make me feel good.

One spring she brought me a small plum tree, about three feet tall. It was the plum tree that we had given her many years ago. We had purchased the plum tree at an auction when it was little more than a twig. The plum tree was a Bradshaw Plum which was my mother's name. My mother was pleased, but the plum twig never grew well and never produced any fruit. She always assumed that it didn't grow well because it was likely a hybrid, and she had no other plums to cross-pollenate it.

We also had green gage plums and she thought it would do better in my yard. So, now it was mine. We planted it together, had some lunch and lemonade and then off she went back to her garden in the city. Three years later, the plum tree had grown three feet and blossomed in the spring. The next year it was twice as high and in full bloom.

In the fall, when my mother came for a visit, we picked a dozen plums for her to take home. In the years that followed, my mother brought many plants and shrubs from her garden. Everything she brought grew large and well. She delivered a small cedar shrub from a neighbour that was scruffy and spindly. Planted outside our bedroom window, it grew to eight feet tall and bushed out to fill the entire corner of the house.

When we left the farm and moved to the city, the Bradshaw Plum was fifteen feet tall and loaded with plums every year. We realized over time that the nutrients in the river silt was what caused the plants to grow exceptionally well. **Lesson Learned!**

The Green Thumb

Although the plants that my mother gave me always grew well, most of them would die in the fall. The plants that I grew never did very well regardless of the river silt in the soil. House plants were particularly reluctant to last very long. My elderly neighbour, grew wonderful gardens with lots of beautiful plants. Whenever I would go to visit and have coffee, I would marvel at the plants outside that lined her house and ringed her trees and shrubs. I was awed at the beautiful hanging baskets and potted plants that adorned her living room and dining room. I often wished I knew how, at her age, she managed to care so very well for all the plants she had inside and out.

I asked her occasionally about which plants grew the best in the sun or the shade. She was always eager to share her knowledge, but it didn't help me much, I just didn't have the knack. I vowed to ask her some day what her secret was.

Eventually, when I was having coffee with her one day, I asked how she managed to keep all those plants so well cared for and what was the secret to her 'green thumb'. She laughed and told me, "My dear, I don't have a 'green thumb'. When they start to wilt or get scruffy, I just throw them out and buy new ones." Since that day I have always had the most beautiful house plants I could find. **Lesson Learned!**

A Neighbour's Shed

When we first met my elderly neighbour's daughter and son-in-law, they lived a few blocks away in a trailer on a different piece of property. After our elderly neighbour and her husband passed away, the daughter and son-in-law moved into her home. As can be expected they made some changes to the old house, the grounds, and small outbuildings.

Eventually, the son-in-law decided to build a new, bigger garden and lawn shed for the lawnmower and garden tools. Rather than make one of his own design, he purchased the plans and supplies from a hardware supply company. He was quite pleased with the decision he had made and had all of the materials and plans delivered to his yard.

It was a big job, and he spent many hours laying a good foundation for the shed. He ran into a problem after the floor was framed, some of the boards for the flooring were too long. He was disappointed. He thought he had purchased a reputable product from a reliable store. Nevertheless, he continued with the construction. He remeasured the boards that were too long and cut them to length.

When the floor was completed, he put up all the walls and the door as planned. He set up the roof trusses and then ran into a new problem. In addition to the floorboards being to long, some of the roof trusses were too short. Now he was really upset with his purchase. However, as he told us the story later, there came a twist to the events.

While talking to another neighbour, the two of them realized what had happened. In his frustration to shorten the too-long floorboards, he had overlooked the fact that when he had unpacked the lumber, he had mixed up a few pieces. When he shortened the floorboards that were too long, he had actually cut up the roof trusses. The roof trusses that were too short were actually just the right length for the floor! He bought some new trusses and finished his shed. **Lesson Learned!**

Country Home Heating

The small house we lived in lacked a lot of essential things like a decent kitchen. It had no closets and one bedroom had only one window. Our daughter and one son, slept in this room. They had plenty of outdoors space to play in and we were never concerned about having only one window in their bedroom.

Apparently our daughter had a different opinion. Our son's bed was against the window, and he was not about to trade sides. Our daughter wanted a window beside her bed. She nagged us about this for a long time. As it happened, Dad worked on a construction site at this time, and he managed to commandeer a relatively nice sized bedroom window. He snuck it home without his daughter seeing it and waited for a sunny weekend.

On a Saturday afternoon, while she happened to be in her room, Dad walked to the back of the house and flashed up his chainsaw. Chainsaws make a lot of noise. Our daughter came running into the backyard to find out what was happening. She got there just in time to see the blade of the chainsaw cut into her bedroom wall. She was shocked and alarmed and screamed at her Dad. Dad just kept on cutting for a few minutes, since he knew he had her attention. Then he turned off the saw and set it down.

He asked her what the problem was. She was almost in tears because he was cutting into her bedroom wall. She wanted to know what he was doing. He said, "Making country home heating, look at all this nice firewood". She was not satisfied with the explanation obviously. He finally told her he was making a hole for her new window. When the window was installed and she was happy again, the wood from the wall was actually used in our wood fireplace as 'country home heating'. **Lesson Learned!**

Pruning The Pear Tree

At the back of the house, in front of the corner nearest the river, and beside our daughter's new window was an old pear tree. The trunk was about ten feet tall. It had many long old branches that bloomed each year and produced a few 'winter' pears in the fall.

With the advent of the new window, a problem arose. In the wind, branches tapped on the window of our daughter's room. Now she wanted the pear tree pruned. We had to agree that the noise from the branches was annoying. The pear tree didn't appear to have been pruned – ever!

Dad would prune the tree was the result of the discussion. The problem with this idea was that Dad had never pruned anything. That shouldn't be too big a deal. With a few discussions on what to trim and where, he would be able to do an adequate job and the pear tree would be the better for it. While I was in town for groceries, without any more discussion, Dad decided to prune the pear tree. When I returned, he was quite pleased with himself and eager to show off his efforts. He definitely pruned the tree. He cut the trunk down to seven feet tall and completely delimbed it. There wasn't a single branch left.

I tried to explain that the tree would never grow back. There would never be any branches or fruit again and he actually thought that was a good idea. Explaining that it was too old and limbless to even grow branches with leaves didn't seem to matter to him.

That pear tree stood there for seven years with only one little four-inch branch with four leaves and never another pear. At some point, Dad realized it was probably not the way to prune the pear tree. **Lesson Learned!**

The Stump Of A Worthless Tree

Over the years there were a few heated words over the fate of the pear tree trunk. As time went on we seemed to forget about it altogether. Dad had a friend who was a woodcarver. He made gorgeous things out of wood. When he came to visit one afternoon, the discussion came around to the pear tree, he had to see it, of course. As far as I knew, nothing came of the conversation.

The tree was still there a few years later. One afternoon I came home from work, and it was gone. Where did it go, I asked Dad. He told me that his friend had called and asked if we wanted to sell the tree. Dad said he didn't have to pay for it, he could just have it if he came and picked it up.

So, his friend arrived, and they cut it down and he took it away. I wasn't happy about not having discussed it first, but it was ugly just standing there doing nothing year after year. It was probably an improvement that it was gone, except for the six-inch stump, which is likely still there. After all it was just the trunk of a worthless tree anyway, right?

As it turns out, it wasn't quite worthless. Dad's friend told us a while later that because it was pear wood, it was actually worth about $700.00! And Dad just gave it to him without asking what it was worth.

As an after-thought, a couple of years later Dad's friend presented me with a beautiful wooden jewellery box, completely carved from the wood of the pear tree. A lovely, thoughtful gift but not worth $700.00. **Lesson Learned!**

A Sunroof To Watch The Weather

While Dad was working with the construction company, they needed to dispose of lots of left-over lumber and we welcomed the chance to stock up on construction materials. He often brought materials home in the trunk of the car, but many times the crew would deliver the excess lumber. We made many improvements to this little old house with the delivered lumber.

Dad loved watching the weather especially during the spring rains and the winter snowstorms. We wanted to enlarge our small bedroom with an alcove built off the river side of the house with some of the lumber and move our bed into it.

The plan was to put windows on all three sides. One on each end and a large window facing the river. We would be able to lay in bed and watch the river go by. Our adventurous spirit peaked and we decided to install a sunroof over the bed, and we would be able to watch the rainfalls and snowfalls all year round. For the most part, the construction went as planned with a little help from our friends. The concept worked very well. We enjoyed many late nights and early mornings laying in bed and watching the river and the weather. The best was yet to come. While we enjoyed a few rainfalls, lightening and thunderstorms, we hadn't yet seen a snowfall.

As winter approached, Dad was anxiously waiting for a snowstorm. There were a few light snowfalls to watch, but he waited impatiently for a really heavy winter snowfall. Finally, the snowfalls hit. Lots of snow! Roads were closed and the whole valley was shut down. When the snow warning came Dad couldn't wait for bedtime. He climbed onto the bed, laid down, and looked up through the sunroof to watch the driving snow. He was thrilled. In the beginning it was exactly what he had waited for.

However, in less than an hour the snow had covered the sunroof completely and he could see no more snow falling. This was not what he had planned. Although we enjoyed many rainstorms as well as some thunder and lightening through the remaining seasons, the snow covered the sunroof for most of the winter every year and Dad was never able to see the snowstorms through the sunroof. **Lesson Learned!**

The Tale Of Three Swimming Pools
Pool #1

Although our children went to the river and the sandbars to swim, and some years had the water in the gully, Dad and I wanted something a little cleaner to stay cool. We purchased a twelve-foot diameter, four foot high, backyard, above ground pool. They are a bit tricky to set up, even if you follow the instructions. It was a family effort, everyone helped. At the end of the season, we disassembled it and stored it for the winter. The following year we set it up in the late spring and took it down again in the fall. The third year it was showing some wear and tear when we assembled it. Parts were getting rusty and some of the supports were a little bent and beat up, but it still held water and lasted well through the summer. Taking the pool apart each fall did not seem to be a good idea. We would need a new pool next year. Pool #1 barely lasted three years. **Lesson Learned!**

Pool #2

We decided to replace the pool in the following spring. Instead of taking the second pool apart each fall, we chose to leave it up at the end of the season with a little less water in it and see how it survived the winter. Leaving the pool standing all winter proved to be a better idea. It survived the next two winters very well. The pool was well on its way to surviving the third year. Until it didn't. The boys were rough-housing in the water one afternoon when one of them slammed up against the side of the pool and that was the end of it. The railing broke apart and the liner split all the way to the bottom. The boys rode the tidal wave out onto the grass as the pool washed about fifteen hundred gallons of pool water into our backyard and basement. Pool #2 lasted almost three years. No more rough-housing allowed in the pool! **Lesson Learned!**

Pool #3

Of course, we needed a new pool in the spring. Being the creative family that we were, we decided to dig out a foot of the backyard lawn and sink the pool down a foot, creating an in-ground base for the new pool. Dad began to install the new pool by himself but had sort of forgotten how to do it. He became quite upset and frustrated. Our kids were older now and decided that they could set up the pool themselves. They took over. They started out ok but soon started squabbling over the process. After everyone had a time-out, we all got together and the pool was installed, filled and functional. This pool was more fun than the previous two. We were pleased with our efforts to dig it into the ground. Late in the second year, when swimming season was ending, it was in decent shape and ready for the third year.

When we came home from work one afternoon, there were fifteen cows standing around the pool drinking the water. The cows were supposed to be in the field across the road but managed to get loose occasionally. In the past, they would wander through our front and back yards and then move on to other places. This time when they had wandered into our backyard and because the pool was lower to the grass, the drinking water was well within their reach, so they took advantage of the handy water supply. The farmer and his help soon showed up and herded them back across the road. We figured that the cows felt that the new lower pool was a new water supply. **Lesson Learned!**

Pool #3 Continued

Many of the cows in the field across the road were pregnant and gave birth while they were in that field. We often heard the cows bellowing in the early morning when they went into labour. Later in the day a new calf could be seen nursing as its life began. New life on a farm is always welcomed, whether it is a calf or a baby bunny.

One afternoon when we arrived home from shopping, we spotted a day-old calf in our backyard laying up against the fence. His mother was nowhere around. We called up the farmer to let him know where his new calf was. We had no idea how he had managed to get there.

The farmer arrived later with his 5-year-old son at his side. As the farmer approached the calf, the calf jumped up and the farmer tried to grab him. The calf was quicker and knocked the farmer over. The farmer was on the ground and his son started to cry because he thought his Dad was hurt. Dad was fine and I took the boy into the house, so he wasn't distracting his Dad and I could keep him calm. We watched through the kitchen window as the farmer chased the calf around the backyard trying to tackle him.

It took a few tries, but finally as the calf ran towards the swimming pool, the farmer lunged and tackled the calf. As they went to the ground they fell against the pool, ripping it open and dumping the water. Neither the farmer nor the calf was hurt but they were wet, and the pool was finished. Pool #3 almost lasted three years. The farmer offered to pay to replace the pool, but we never did. Life expectancy of above ground swimming pools is less than three years. **Lesson Learned!**

The Hidden Advantage To
A Riding Lawn Mower

Mowing the lawns on a third of an acre of backyard and front yard is time consuming and tiring. When we first moved onto our farm the yards were not well kept and the only lawn mower we had was an old push mower. Mowing all that yard, front and back took several days and was a constant chore that no one wanted to do. We eventually acquired a used electric lawn mower. It was better and took less time. But with the cord attached all the time, the kids were continually running over the cord. This was not a viable choice. We discussed a riding mower but after talking about it, we decided that it wasn't a good idea since our boys would surely ruin it or try to turn it into a sportier model.

We finally bought a regular power mower. After our children grew up and moved on we talked again about buying a riding mower. Dad was happy with the power mower and didn't want to pay the price of a riding mower. Eventually, he relented, and we shopped for a riding mower, but he was not convinced that it was necessary. I promised him he could have a little trailer with it to help with the livestock feed and firewood, which sealed the deal.

In the early spring, before the grass started to grow, we purchased a riding lawn mower, with the trailer. Dad was impressed at how much easier and quicker it was to do all that mowing. He soon had it down to a science and he actually looked forward to mowing. Our lawns began to look like parklands. Mowing was obviously more frequent in the spring and early summer, but the grass grew slower towards the end of summer and the fall.

However, mowing in late summer and early fall when the fruit trees started to produce their fruit took on a new meaning. Dad gained a new respect for the riding mower. He rearranged his mowing route. As he drove around the yards, he was able to pick fresh plums and apples right off the branches, without slowing down. He loved it and looked forward to every mowing day! **Lesson Learned!**

Lawn Mowing After A Car Race

Dad didn't just mow the lawn like everyone else. He wore a helmet, mostly for fun, and fired up a cassette player and plugged in his ear plugs (there were no iPhones then), turned on the mower and away he went. I noticed occasionally that when his music was lively he went a little faster. Our lawns were flat, mostly, so it wasn't a problem. However, a portion of the lawn sloped down along the riverbank, so I cautioned him to be careful on the slope as he mowed along the river. I thought that he was having far too much fun with all the fruit and the music, but he was mowing our lawns beautifully, so I didn't nag him about it.

Time past and all was going smoothly, until one Sunday when he watched a car race before he mowed the lawn. He was a race fan and often watched Nascar and the like on Sundays, but he didn't usually mow the lawn afterwards. This particular Sunday, after the car race, he decided to mow the lawn.

He donned his helmet, his music and started to mow the lawn. I checked on him from time to time and noticed that his technique had changed a little. I eventually caught onto what he was doing. He was mowing the lawn as if the lawn were a racetrack and the mower was a race car. He was going too fast. At first I was amused, after all the yard was flat, what harm could it do?

A little later I looked out and he was running along the riverbank from side to side and occasionally the mower would tip to the river side and two wheels would come off the ground. This was dangerous. If he rolled over, he and the mower would end up in the river. I ran outside and flagged him down. I told him to stop and get off the riverbank.

He put the mower away for the day and when he came into the house, I had a few choice words for the 'race car' driver. He realized how careless he had been on the riverbank, and he promised that he would never mow the lawn 'after a car race' again. And he never did. **Lesson Learned!**

Lightening On The Dike

In order to leave our property, we drove up and over the dike which had been built after the 1948 flood. Our property was between the dike and the river, so we were not protected. Along the top of the dike, a road ran all the way around the island where we lived. The farmers in the area had built gates along the dike to keep their cattle in the fields. Under the gates they installed metal cattle guards as well. The dirt roads at the top of the dikes were considerably higher than the properties the dike protected, including ours.

In the summertime, as everywhere else, we had some fabulous thunder and lightening storms. Most of the time there was so much wind and rain that we watched the storms from inside the house. During our early years on the farm, there were often spectacular storms far away to the west. Living below the dike, surrounded by the river and lots of trees, we could not see the distant storms.

On occasion we would stand on top of the dike by the cattle gate and watch the distant lightening shows off to the west. It was a perfect location, and the views were spectacular. One late summer evening we watched the storm to the west as it approached our area. The rain hadn't started so we stayed longer than we probably should have.

Eventually the lightening was getting closer, and the show got better and better. Then came a lightening strike that we could actually feel. We instantly realized that we were making a big mistake. There were a couple tall trees in the fields nearby, but we were not only the highest point on the dike, but we were leaning on a metal gate and standing on a metal cattle guard! If we didn't leave we could easily be struck by the lightening that was flashing close enough for us to feel it! We left immediately and were a lot more careful during future storms. **Lesson Learned!**

A Cadillac Chicken Carrier

We owned several dogs over the years and the biggest one was a Saint Bernard. We also had at this time, a deaf, Blue Roan Cocker Spaniel named Royce. When you have a small dog named after a Rolls Royce, then naturally your Saint Bernard's name is Cadillac, what else!

Cadillac was a beautiful and very friendly puppy who grew into a beautiful, friendly, very, large dog. He loved all the animals on the farm, as did the rest of our pets. One of his favourite pastimes became carrying chickens around the backyard. He never hurt them, he just liked to carry them around. We could not understand how or why he did this. Like a lot of other things we learned, we decided to pay close attention to the events to see how this worked.

Cadillac would, very carefully, pick up his chicken of choice by closing his teeth over the middle of the chickens back bone. The chicken never tried to escape as he put his paw on the tail feathers and fastened onto the backbone. In this way he was able to carry the chicken all over the back-yard without hurting it. However, every so often he would walk over to our picnic table and set the chicken on the bench of the table and without letting go, he would adjust his grip, or so it appeared, and then carry on with his adventure. But why was he doing this?

He would continually walk the perimeter of the yard and it seemed that he would randomly stop for a few minutes, take a look around and then carry on to the next spot until he had had enough or got tired of the game and let the chicken go. We were still puzzled as to what he was doing or why. After some kitchen table discussion, the only thing we could think of was that perhaps he was trying to dig a hole and bury the chicken.

As he worked his way around the yard, he would occasionally stop and you could almost see him looking at the ground and thinking, "How can I dig a hole here without letting go of my chicken?" And then he would move to the next spot and repeat the same procedure. Cadillac seemed to enjoy this game and did it often. We are still amazed that a Saint Bernard could carry chickens without hurting them. **Lesson Learned!**

Cadillac's Jacket

Our younger son and Cadillac, the Saint Bernard, loved to scuffle in the backyard. They spent hours chasing each other and wrestling around. In our porch there hung a big blue jacket that originally belonged to Dad. Our son would put on this blue jacket whenever he played with Cadillac to protect his clothes from dirt and tears and his arms from scratches. It became a sign to Cadillac that it was playtime! If our son went into the backyard without the jacket, Cadillac would greet him as he did everyone else. But that jacket meant playtime.

When our son came home from school, he would put on the jacket, walk out the door, open the gate and was immediately knocked down by Cadillac. Cadillac was huge. On his hind legs, he could put his front paws on Dad's shoulders and look him straight in the eye. He weighed about 180 pounds. Our son was a young teenager weighing about 95 pounds, so Cadillac always had the upper hand. The whole family watched the two of them and their antics from time to time, but we had no idea that the blue jacket was that important.

One Saturday afternoon in early winter, our oldest son decided to venture out to see the livestock. Since the weather had turned chilly, he grabbed Dad's blue jacket from the hook in the porch. He went out the back door, through the gate into the backyard. He took about six steps past the corner of the house; Cadillac saw the jacket and our son was bowled over by Cadillac in full charge! The jacket obviously meant playtime, no matter who was wearing it. **Lesson Learned!**

The Pet Bunny

When our daughter made a pet out of a baby bunny, the bunny lived in her bedroom, in a cage, most of the time and especially at night. She was responsible for the care of the bunny, the cleaning of the cage and other messes which occasionally resulted from having a bunny as a pet.

While the bunny was small she carried it everywhere. It was very tame and in the beginning they were inseparable. But bunnies grow into rabbits and become a bit too heavy to carry all the time, so she bought a cat collar and a leash. Pretty soon the rabbit was trained to accept the collar and leash and long walks became an event. The rabbit was quite attached to our daughter, and they were able to play in the backyard without the leash. The rabbit was a big hit at "Show and Tell" at school. He was a big fluffy friendly "bunny" that allowed and enjoyed lots of petting.

By the time the rabbit was about a year old, he had earned the right to investigate the house and was often allowed out of his cage during the summer days when there was no school. It was our daughter's responsibility to see that he didn't get into any trouble. He loved his freedom to explore everywhere. Most of the time he was a fun addition. Occasionally, he would disappear and there would be a frantic search and sometimes tears, until he was found. Once in a while he would escape out the back door and could be quite elusive, with a whole farmyard to explore and hide.

Eventually his antics started to become more of a chore than a game, as most kids usually discover. We started experiencing some problems in the house with the phone, and the stereo which were narrowed down to rabbit chewed wires. About the same time our daughter was losing interest in her pet rabbit. Eventually, he was banished to the rabbit pens and only visited occasionally. Bunnies make cute pets for little girls, but rabbits take a lot of care and do not belong in the house. **Lesson Learned!**

A Mole & A Blind Cat

Our second son had a black cat named "Kitt" after the car in the television show "Knight Rider" because the cat was black like the car, and he liked the show. Kitt was a normal cat for the first few years, but he developed some strange behaviors as he got older.

At first, the most noticeable attitude was how he approached eating. He would not eat out of his dish unless it was full. This was odd but easy to deal with. Something else that seemed strange was that he refused to use the litter box he had always used. He did not make messes around the house, instead he actually used the toilet. This, too, was strange but not a problem that needed changing.

Eventually, though we noticed another problem. We had a German Shepherd that liked to sleep near the doorway between the living room and the kitchen so that he could see what was going on. Kitt started bumping into him on a regular basis. Finally, we decided that Kitt might not be able to see and off to the vet for a check up. Sure enough, Kitt was blind from cataracts. That diagnosis answered a few questions.

Kitt couldn't see food in his bowl and when the food was low, his whiskers couldn't 'see' the food either, so he didn't think there was any food in the bowl. The same principle applied to the litter box, but Kitt had solved that problem himself even though we had no idea how he figured it out. Cataract surgery was way beyond our budget and therefore the cat remained blind for the rest of his long life. Kitt taught himself to cope in his own way with how to get around the yard. He learned the boundaries and seldom got lost. When he got confused he just stood his ground and meowed until someone rescued him.

During his adventures in the back yard, he found a mole hill. We realized that he knew what it was because he could obviously smell the mole and possibly feel the mole scurrying underground. He staked out that mole hill for days. We thought the poor cat was in a futile pursuit because he was blind, he would never catch a mouse, let alone a mole underground. Within four days, he caught and killed the mole and actually moved on to another mole hill elsewhere in the yard. He didn't catch all of the moles he stalked but he caught many. We greatly underestimated this blind cat. **Lesson Learned!**

Cat In The Window

Our children all had cats. It was a promise we made to them when we moved to the country. Our oldest son's cat was black and white and was called "Boots", because, of course, he had white feet. Boots liked to sit in our west-facing bedroom window and soak up the afternoon sun. We were away one afternoon, but our son was home and in the other room. Boots was on the windowsill as usual. If you were to look out our bedroom window you would see a bit of the river, the roadway down to the river that ran in front of the house and the huge, tall aspens that lined the river. Some of the aspens were 100 feet tall. Eagles and hawks lived in these trees every year.

Something happened while we were out. Our son who was in the room across the hall with the door closed, remembered hearing what he thought was a gunshot but thought nothing of it because the farmers shoot vermin on a regular basis. When we got home we were shocked to find that the bedroom window had been smashed to pieces. It was a double paned window, and it was gone. There were shards of glass all over the bed, the floor, and the dresser. There was also blood and shards of glass embedded in the bedroom door, which was in the opposite corner of the room, about twelve feet away.

At first we were in total shock. As we looked around, we checked under the bed. There under the bed was the cat, in possession of one exceptionally large and very dead hawk! It became obvious that the hawk, high in the aspens to the west, had spotted the cat in the window. His hunting instincts took over and he dive-bombed the cat, not knowing it was on the other side of a window. Luckily, the cat was unhurt.

The force that the diving hawk exerted, carried it through the double paned window and clear across the room until it and some of the glass hit the bedroom door. We aren't sure what killed the hawk, going through the window or the force with which it struck the door. One or the other, or maybe both, killed it. It may have lived long enough to flop around and excite the cat which may be how it got under the bed. It was considerably larger than the cat. Nevertheless, the cat was guarding a dead hawk when we came home.

The gun shot that our son had heard was likely the hawk going through the window or hitting the door. We would have thought the hawk could have hit the window, but we wouldn't have thought it possible for a hawk to go through the double-paned glass. A year later we were still finding glass shards in the dresser drawers which were closed at the time. **Lesson Learned!**

Ye Olde Hydro Meter

About two years after we had moved into our small farmhouse, the hydro company knocked on our door. Apparently, the hydro company decided that our hydro meter was too old because our hydro bill was too low. We, of course, thought $35.00 per month was fine. After all, who was going to complain about low hydro bills. In any case, the hydro company was going to install a new meter, at no cost to us, which was also a good thing. The new meter was soon installed, and life went on.

The first month with the new meter appeared to be an "adjustment period" because our hydro bill was about $15.00 lower than the previous bill. For the next few months, the bill stayed at around $20 to $25. Finally, we called the hydro company, concerned that there was an error and we would eventually get hit with a higher bill when it was adjusted. The accounting department said that our bill was as recorded.

However, the person in accounting was concerned at the drop in our account and agreed that the amount did seem to be too low. She forwarded our call to the technical department. After several transfers and lots of explanations from us, we were finally transferred to a technician who was able to check the work order and current records. Apparently, the new meter was working fine. The subsequent hydro recordings were lower.

The hydro company had been incorrect about our old bills being too low as the rates recorded on the new meter indicated that the old meter rates had been too high. The technician said he was pleased, and surprised, to report that our hydro bills had been reduced to reflect the new lower monthly readings. The hydro company had been too quick to make sure that we weren't getting away with paying too little for our electricity. They should have left us with the old meter. **Lesson Learned!**

Home Electricity Study

In Grade IV, our daughter was asked to figure out how much electricity her family used by reporting on the family's appliances. The next day in class, the teacher advised her that her numbers were much too low and that she hadn't listed enough appliances. She was asked to go home and make another list of all the appliances that her family used.

At that time, in that old farmhouse, we had only the essentials. The wiring was very old and the whole house ran on just one fuse. We had a minimum of appliances. We used an old, manual wringer washing machine and all the laundry was hung on a clothesline to dry. The fridge was ancient and tiny. We cooked on an old wood stove. The house was heated with a small furnace, similar to the ones you would find in a small mobile home. In the winter, extra heat came from a wood fireplace. We had one small television with an outside antenna and no cablevision. There was only one light bulb and one socket in each room.

Most recreational cabins at the time, used more electricity than we did! Back in class the next day, our daughter presented to her teacher her list of all our household appliances, a copy of our hydro bill and a letter from her mother stating that it was an accurate list. The teacher studied the list and the hydro bill and read the letter, then apologised to our daughter for doubting her. **Lesson Learned!**

Rural Cablevision

Cablevision was a relatively new innovation when we moved to the country. As the years went by more cablevision installations were supplied to residences. However, rural communities were largely ignored. The argument was that it was too costly to supply and maintain because the rural areas were not populated enough. Regulations eventually changed and the cable companies were ordered to supply cable to most rural areas, including our area.

By now our children were feeling a little left out because almost everyone at school had cablevision except them. Saying they were excited to learn that cablevision was coming down their street was putting it mildly. As the date approached for the laying of the cable, we were concerned that the rest of the residences had been contacted by the cable company, but we had not. Maybe they didn't know we lived here since it was out of sight of the rest of the road.

We made a call to the cable company and expressed our concern. They would look into it and get back to us. When they called back, they explained that because we were on the river side of the dike, we would not be getting cablevision. The cable was being buried in the ground and they were not permitted to dig into the dike, therefore, they could not run the cable to our house.

We checked out the diking regulations in the bylaws governing our area. The regulations were specific. The dangers from erosion, prohibited any disturbance of the surface of the dike, period! We now had three extremely disappointed children in our house, and it appeared there was nothing we could do about it. As parents, we had often made the impossible happen, but it didn't appear that we could create a miracle in this instance.

The day arrived when they started on the cable, the children whined a lot. A few days later, the man digging a trench and laying the cable was at the last house by the dike as I drove home. I stopped at my mailbox and when I got out of the car, I greeted him and asked, almost jokingly, when he was coming over the dike to our house. He turned to me and said that he would be there within the hour, and he was. By the time the kids got home from school, the cable was installed.

The next day, a technician showed up to hook it up for us. He explained that we were incredibly lucky. The guy who ran the line through the dike did not know that he wasn't allowed to dig through the dike, so he just ran the cable. The cable company figured it was better to accept it and hook us up, than to cause trouble by removing it. Another family miracle created. **Lesson Learned!**

Loss Of The Wood Cook Stove

The old wood cook stove that was in the kitchen when we purchased the property was a beautiful white stove made by a company called Matus. It had everything a wood cook stove should have. We used a wood cook stove in the past and were thrilled to have this beauty. If you ever cooked with wood you know nothing cooks as well as wood. This stove needed a little work as some non-essential parts of it did not work anymore. In town, there was a shop that sold and repaired old wood stoves. When we decided to get some parts repaired, we went to the owner to discuss our needs.

The owner of the shop had never heard of a Matus wood cook stove, so he did some checking. It was indeed a rare stove, but the parts that he would need were common. He suggested that we bring the stove in, and he would look it over and give us an estimate of the repairs and the time it would take. Regardless of the repairs, parts would take time to acquire. He suggested that we make other arrangements for cooking, while he repaired it.

We purchased a cheap electric stove for the interim. Wood cook stoves are extremely heavy and difficult to move. We loaded the stove into the trailer and delivered it to the shop. The owner admired the stove and promised to give us a quote in a week or two. We left, pleased to have made the choice to get it repaired, but sad to not be able to use it for a while. We waited patiently for our quote.

Two, then three weeks went past but the owner had not called. We called the shop, no answer. We left messages, no answer. We were growing concerned, so we drove to the shop. The shop was still there and so was the owner. He remembered us but said he knew nothing about us bringing in a stove. He told us to look around the shop and show him our stove. The stove was not there, anywhere. He said that he had never heard of a Matus stove. We were dumbfounded! He asked to see the work order for the stove. We didn't have one, obviously. We didn't even have a receipt. He stood his ground and refused to acknowledge that such a stove even existed. We finally gave up and left.

We did talk to the police about the possible theft of our stove. The owner was known to them. There had been other reports of problems with the owner but nothing that could be substantiated. They were sympathetic but unable to do anything since we didn't even have a receipt or a workorder. We didn't even have a picture of the stove. The stove was never found and never returned to us. **Lesson Learned!**

Sometimes Children Listen Too Well

You try, as a parent, to teach your children to do things that will help them and protect them as they grow. You try to teach them not to talk to strangers, not to eat wild berries or mushrooms they don't know and to stand still when bees or wasps are buzzing around them. The bees or wasps will likely fly away. Experience shows that this works most of the time and children usually listen.

Our older son, often spent his Saturdays with the farmer's son who lived a few fields away from our house. They would play around the farm all day, doing whatever boys do. At the end of the day, he would come home by taking a short cut through the farmyard and across the fields. One such day he headed home around the back of one of the barns and walked across a stack of old lumber as he headed for the field.

At some point, he stepped on a board and disturbed a large wasps' nest. As the wasps swarmed around him, instead of running away from the wasps, he did exactly what his mother told him. He stood perfectly still. By the time he got home his head was covered in wasp stings, his face was all puffy and he had tears streaming down his face.

After we treated all the stings, changed his clothes, and calmed him down, he told us what had happened. He told us he tried to do what Mom had told him and just stand still, but there were wasps all around him and they just kept stinging him, so he finally had to run. We explained to him that he had disturbed a wasp's nest and he should have run right away. Sometimes children listen too well. **Lesson Learned!**

Lots Of Wasps' Nests

The summer after we moved in, we noticed that there were lots of wasps around. Being on the lookout for wasps' nest was ongoing. They were elusive and we didn't find any in the early years. There were many weeks when we could not use the front door because of the large numbers of wasps on the veranda. There didn't appear to be any wasps' nests there, at least we couldn't find any.

There were wasps at the back of the house also. Our German Shepherd had a bad habit of trying to bite the wasps that flew close to the back wall of the house. He often ended the day with many wasp stings on his face and mouth, but he never quit.

When we decided to renovate the kitchen east wall which faced the backyard, we tore out the panelling on the inside of the wall. Next morning there were wasps all over the kitchen. This continued for several days. We finally lined the wall with plastic to keep the wasps out of the kitchen. We would sit at the kitchen table and listen to the ping, ping, ping as the wasps hit the plastic trying to get through.

It was late fall when we started to redo the walls in the back porch. As we started to remove the panelling that covered the wall, we finally knew where the wasps were coming from. In taking down the panels we uncovered a huge four-foot by four-foot wasps' nest inside the wall. All the wasps were gone luckily, but the nest was in one piece. Subsequent renovations proved the theory that all the outer walls of the house, the roof over the veranda and probably most of the attic contained large wasp nests. As long as the house remained standing, there would be lots of wasps and lots of wasps' nests. **Lesson Learned!**

Company Coming - Check The Sofa

We loved our house in the country. It was old, likely built in 1935 or earlier based on a piece of newspaper in the walls. It had a mostly dirt basement and an incomplete foundation. We often had moles and mice in the basement. Traps were set constantly and highly effective at catching mice, but we had no way to stop them permanently unless we sealed the basement. That was an unlikely prospect.

Since the house was so old, mice regularly made their way upstairs as well. We sealed every opening we could find, but mice are small and can make their way around through holes you would think are far too small. All of our food was in sealed containers to protect it and to help discourage the mice. No food, no mice, we hoped. Try as we did we never completely won the battle.

Our children often had friends sleep over and we had a fold-out sofa to make up for them. Usually, we knew they were coming ahead of time and the bed would be made up and ready for them at bedtime. The bed would be stripped, and the bedding washed when they left. Lots of friends slept in that sofa and lots of friends slept on the floor in sleeping bags.

Saturday nights could see six or seven teenagers sleeping on the floor. Eventually the kids moved away to town and Saturday night became 'parents' night', no kids allowed. We had close friends who often came on Saturday and stayed the night.

One Saturday they came, and they decided at the last minute to stay the night. The bed hadn't been made up. We brought out the bedding and opened the sofa bed. There at the head of the bed, settled in nice and cozy, was a momma mouse and five newly born babies. What a shock! We might have been horrified, but our friends were as used to the country as we were.

We scooped up the momma and babies and put them in a box outside. We washed down the bed, put on the sheets, gave our guests our bed and settled in for a good nights' sleep with a good laugh and not another thought. However, we made a new house rule: Company coming - check the sofa! **Lesson Learned!**

The Electric Mouse Trap

In keeping with our efforts to eliminate the mice from our house, nothing was out of the question. We often spent our evenings brainstorming solutions to the problems we faced on many fronts. One such discussion turned to a better mouse trap. We had good workable mouse traps, but more is better and new might be even better. Since, between the two of us, Dad and I had great creative ideas, we decided to put them to work.

We came up with an idea for an electric mouse trap. In the evenings when we were sitting at the table talking, the occasional mouse would run across the top of the stove on its way to a mouse trap, we hoped. We concluded that we could put an electric mouse trap on the stove and that it could then be plugged into the stovetop outlet. Now we just had to rig a regular mouse trap to an electrical circuit. Dad having electrical training was a whiz at electrical tinkering. The wiring was easy enough, but we also needed an on/off switch so that the mouse was the only thing that got zapped. The switch was installed, and the circuit was tested. Now all we needed was a lot of patience and a volunteer mouse.

Later in the evening, when the house grew dark, we made coffee, baited the trap with strong cheddar cheese and turned off the lights. Once our eyes adjusted to the darkness, Dad plugged in the trap, turned the switch to the "on" position and we settled in to wait for the mouse to volunteer to walk across the stove and onto the trap. Mice don't arrive on cue.

We finally turned on the lights at 3 am, turned off the trap, unplugged it and went to bed. We had to repeat this procedure three different nights before we got lucky, and a mouse volunteer showed up. He climbed onto the top of the stove, wandered around a little and finally found the trap. In seconds he stepped onto the trap, reached for the bait and the trap went off. The electricity zapped him, and he flew through the air, landing on the floor clear across the kitchen.

Unfortunately for us, and fortunately for him, it didn't kill him. The zap hardly even slowed him down. He was on his little feet in seconds and disappeared behind the nearest cupboard before we could even move. The electric mouse trap really worked; it just didn't kill mice. **Lesson Learned!**

Alternate School Bullies

When our children first started school in this area, the school bus didn't come past our street. Although it wasn't a particularly long way to walk, it was a busy road. Driving the kids to the bus stop became part of the daily ritual.

When we were intending to buy the house, we noticed a small school just a short way down the road and thought that our children would be attending that school. Unfortunately, the school was no longer in regular school use.

Shortly after our children started school, there appeared to be a small number of older students attending the school. After a few questions, we were informed that the classes held there were for 'alternate' students who were unruly in regular classes and were therefore, bused to this small school for more individual attention. It seemed like a promising idea for the students.

As the days went by and we drove past the school, things changed. The students would see us coming down the road and stand in front of the car and harass us. We usually managed to get past them, but they were very rude and rough. They would call us names and pound or kick at the car. They weren't dangerous, just loud, and abusive.

Our children were afraid of them every morning. The 'alternate students' left their school in the early afternoon, so they were only there when we went by in the morning. They were just being bullies. We would have to find a way to deal with the problem. We talked to our children and told them this, but it didn't help, and the harassment continued almost every day.

While baking cookies one day, I decided to make two extra dozen for the students at the special school. There were about eight students and a teacher, two dozen would do. I told the kids what we were going to do. They didn't think they deserved the cookies. I explained that if we did something nice for them, maybe they would leave us alone. The kids agreed that it was worth a try.

Next morning, we put the cookies in a nice cookie tin and set off for the bus. When the students stepped out in front of us, I rolled down the window and offered them the tin of cookies. They made a few nasty remarks, but they took the cookies and let us pass without anymore trouble. We had an occasional confrontation in the days that followed but they were quite subdued.

When Hallowe'en rolled around, we made up bags of candies for each of them. They actually said thank you. There were no more morning harassments, and they were actually waving at us, and the kids waved back. Every holiday during the year, we brought them treats.

Even when the new school year started, they were friendly. We guessed that word had gotten around. The alternate school students were no longer bullying us and our children learned one way to handle bullies. **Lesson Learned!**

A Bad Hair Day

All girls and women have 'bad hair' days. Adult women can deal with the situation, but young girls, especially teenagers, are particularly devastated. As a mom, a bad hair day in a daughter can cause untold anguish and problems. A bad hair day, on a school day is frustrating.

The morning started out fine, then slowly worsened. We managed to cope through breakfast but going out the door to head for the school bus was almost a tantrum. The boys gave up, got on their bicycles, and left. My daughter was beside herself in frustration and tears. At this point, nothing was going to be good enough to settle her down. Her hair looked fine to me, was definitely the wrong thing to say and the reaction was total hysteria. Her response was that I just didn't understand.

Time was running out if she was going to make the bus. Our children had always had good grades and excellent attendance at school, so I made the best decision I had ever made for my daughter. I suggested that maybe she would rather just take the day off and stay home. Oh boy, was she ever happy! Problem solved. Her hair wasn't any better, but she didn't have to look bad at school. It made me a real hero in her eyes. She is the mom of three girls herself, now and she has never forgotten how her mom solved her 'bad hair day'. **Lesson Learned!**

The Tooth

Although our children were close in age, being two boys and one girl did not make them the best of friends all the time. All siblings have difficulties getting along. As the kids grew older the everyday things and personalities drew them even more apart. Sometimes they thought they hated each other. The boys teased each other but together they would harass and tease their sister to the point that she was certain they hated her. Once in a while, events happen that renews your faith in the closeness of your children, regardless of how they act towards each other.

In their teen years, the school bus route had changed and now picked them up at the end of our street. Most of the school year, when the weather was good, they rode their bicycles to the end of the street and left them there when the bus arrived. One morning nearing the end of the road, our daughter applied the brakes on her bicycle, and they locked up, flipping the bicycle and her forward and throwing our daughter, face first onto the roadway in front of the bicycle. The boys missed the school bus to bring her home. She was crying and her face and arms were bloody and scraped badly. The boys were horrified to see her all banged up. We cleaned her up and took another look. She wasn't as badly scraped as she first looked. However, she had lost her front tooth. A discussion followed and the boys wanted to go to school, so I drove them to school, then came home and made a dentist appointment.

Our daughter was terribly upset that she had lost a tooth, especially the front one. As a teenager, I could understand her upset and tried to convince her that it would be alright. The boys came home from school, dropped their things in the porch and announced that they were going to the end of the road to find the tooth so the dentist could put it back. I warned them that they probably wouldn't be able to find the tooth and even if they did, the dentist may not be able to reinsert it. They didn't care, they were going to try.

It took them more than two hours, but when they came home they had the tooth. The dentist couldn't insert the tooth of course and our daughter ended up with an artificial tooth that looked great. She found out that day, that no matter how much they acted like they hated her, her brothers really did love her. **Lesson Learned!**

Barn Cats Are Not Pets

Our second oldest son loved animals, especially his pets and took great care of them. While working in the garage one afternoon, he noticed that one of the neighbour's barn cats had settled into a corner. He thought that perhaps he should return it to the neighbour's barn. He reached over and picked up the cat, but the cat did not want to be picked up and attacked him, biting his arm just above the wrist. Our son immediately dropped the cat, and it took off for parts unknown.

He came into the house, and we cleaned and bandaged the wound. He was old enough now to have a driver's licence and a car, so we told him to go to emergency and get a tetanus shot. He did and then off he went to party. It was New Year's Eve; a cat bite was not going to slow him down.

A couple of hours later, he called us to say that he was back at the hospital. The doctor he had seen earlier said that it was just a small puncture wound and nothing to worry about and now he had a black line running up his arm. He had blood poisoning. They were admitting him to emergency to administer large doses of antibiotics through an IV drip which would take about an hour.

The doctor explained that he would need large doses every two to three hours all night. Not wishing to miss the New Year's Eve that he and his girl friend had planned, he discussed his options with the doctor. If he didn't have any alcohol and if he promised to come back to the hospital every two hours, he could leave and go back to the party.

He left emergency with the IV tubing still in his arm. He kept his promise to the doctor, and went back every two hours, all night but he was able to attend his party. A New Year's Eve he will never forget. He also will remember that barn cats are not pets! **Lesson Learned!**

Wrapping Christmas Presents

Young teenagers can drive you to a frenzy at times. Christmas was a constant challenge. They each had their own opinion of where they wanted to have Christmas dinner. They all had significant others to spend Christmas with. Some of the time they would go to other families for dinner and sometimes they would invite their girlfriend (boyfriend) to our house. Occasionally there was a friend whose parents were away for Christmas, so they were invited. Either way was fine with us but they just couldn't make up their minds until about Christmas Eve.

Christmas Eve, our teenagers were allowed to open one gift each and the remainder was for Christmas day. They were all 'snoopers' and would try to find the unwrapped gifts ahead of time. We lived in a small house so hiding gifts was a challenge. We decided to wrap and label the gifts as soon as we bought them in order to foil the snoopers. Some were hidden in the attic, some in the trunk of the car, and any other places we could find. Approaching Christmas Eve, the gifts were put under the tree and our young teenagers knew which was theirs. Then they started guessing and trying to peek under the wrapping. It was very hard to surprise them with gifts they had already half-opened.

The final straw came one Christmas, while we were out shopping. The two boys got together and literally unwrapped their gifts and rewrapped them before we got home. We found out about this months later and vowed to put a stop to the snooping.

As the next Christmas rolled around we decided to try a new tactic. When the gifts were under the tree, there were no names on any of the gifts. They were baffled. How could they snoop if none of the gifts were labelled? They could not figure out what we were up to. On Christmas Eve we gave each one a gift meant for them. There were still lots of unmarked presents under the tree and they had no idea which one was for who.

Christmas morning, one of the kids was chosen to hand out the gifts but would have to bring each gift to me to identify who it was for. Our teenagers, as smart as they were, never figured out how we knew who the parcels were for. No more snooping or rewrapping.

Years later when they had moved into their own homes, we broke down and told them how we knew. We had marked each parcel with small dots in a corner: one dot for the oldest son, two for the younger, three for our daughter and a star for guests. **Lesson Learned!**

Aspens Top Themselves

While living on this beautiful piece of property for many years, we were always concerned about the tall aspens that grew along the riverbank at the side of the house. Their root structure was very shallow making them susceptible to windfall. Most people might say that we were worrying about nothing, but we had to live there. One of the things that we had in common, as a couple, was that we both hated the threats presented by high winds and tall trees.

There were three aspens in particular that we wanted removed. After a fierce windstorm forced us to sleep in the living room because we were afraid of the trees falling on our bedroom, we contacted a tree cutting company. Unfortunately, there was nothing they could do because the trees were on the riverbank, not on our property. Apparently, you can't cut down the trees on any riverbank without government approval.

We sent for the government paperwork to get the approval to remove the trees. The paperwork required us to have an arborist's inspection of the trees to prove that they were in danger of falling on our house and thereby an actual threat. So, we called an arborist. We explained to the arborist that we wanted approval to remove the extremely tall aspens on the riverbank and that the government required an inspection. The arborist understood what we needed but told us that it would cost us $250.00 for the assessment and in the end she would not agree to cutting them down. She suggested that we save our money because it wasn't going to happen.

Frustrated, we asked why she would not approve the request without even assessing the trees. Her 'famous last words' were: "Aspens don't fall, they top themselves". Five years later a huge windstorm struck the whole west coast and brought the three aspens down on our house. The aspens fell from the roots up. They tore our whole veranda right off the front of our house, broke several windows and put twenty-four holes in the roof of the house. Many of the drywall seams inside the house were also split and when the trees landed they smashed onto top of the propane tank outside and we lost a full season of propane. Aspens may 'top themselves', but they can also be blown down in a fierce wind. **Lesson Learned!**

Sold!

After the trees came down, our insurance repaired most of the damage, but our home was never the same. Our children had all moved away with their pets. We were planning to go back to work, so as each summer approached we had less and less farm animals. Our last dog passed away and we did not get another.

Then we had a year when the Fraser River rose to unusually high levels and we were once again under flood threat and had actually received our first and only emergency evacuation alert. In preparation, we sold whatever livestock remained. The flood did not reach our property.

Since we were getting older, we decided it was time to move closer to town and the Doctors' offices. We called in a Real Estate agent. We purchased our acre for a small amount, by today's standards, twenty four years ago, but we knew that the location would make it hard to sell because it was outside of the dike. No bank would carry a mortgage on this property; however, we expected that the listing price would be low enough to encourage a sale.

Our Real Estate agent was a gentleman we knew from years past. He was impressed with how lovely the property looked and referred to it as very 'parklike'. However, the house was old and needed painting. We were in shock when he suggested a listing price ten times what we had paid for it when we bought it. We did not believe it would sell for that much, but that's what he wanted to start at, so we agreed.

Many people came and went. Most people would say they could get a mortgage, or they knew 'a guy' at the bank. Some people came back with other creative ideas or offered a trade for the property. Interest in our property continued for several months but no sale was made. In the meantime, we went to our workplace and in the evenings we discussed our options on where we would live if the property sold and what we would do if it did not sell.

Our Real Estate agent was run off his feet. People were coming almost every day to make offers. On the weekends there would be three or four groups there to view the property. We could hardly keep up. Most of the offers fell through due to the mortgage issues they were warned about. One of our neighbours actually called the Real Estate office to complain the house was not worth the asking price and was listed too high. There were a few problems, and it took several months, but finally it was done and we had a sale.

Our Real Estate agent told us that his office was amazed; they had never had a property generate this much activity. They told us the interest was due to the beautiful location, size of the property and the fact that it was so well cared for that it looked like a park. **Sold!** The sales price was almost ten times our original purchase price. **Lesson Learned!**

Retirement

Once our property was sold, we moved into a condo in town. A couple of years later, we sold our business to our second son and his wife.

We are now officially retired and still learning. We miss the 'little white house' that we had dreamed about so many years before, as well as the farming and the livestock. Our children and our ten grandchildren live close by.

We never returned to the little white house we left behind. Eventually the kids all went back to see the farm where they had lived for twenty-five years. They informed us of the changes and showed us pictures, but that was as close as we came to visiting.

I had grown up all over Canada and lived in many places. I always missed not having a place to grow up and call my childhood home. I was pleased that we had finally settled in one place and were able to give our children a house that they could call their childhood home filled with so many happy memories.

THE END

9 781039 182660